HANDICAPPING AMERICA

Handicapping America

BARRIERS TO DISABLED PEOPLE

FRANK BOWE

1817

HARPER & ROW, PUBLISHERS

NEW YORK

HAGERSTOWN

SAN FRANCISCO

LONDON

For my wife, Phyllis, and my daughter, Doran,
with all my love

FIRST EDITION

Designed by Sidney Feinberg

Library of Congress Cataloging in Publication Data

Bowe, Frank G.
   Handicapping America.
   Bibliography: p.
   Includes index.
   1. Handicapped—United States. I. Title.
HV1553.B68   1978   362.4'0973   77-11816
ISBN 0-06-010422-8

78 79 80 81 82 10 9 8 7 6 5 4 3 2 1

Contents

Foreword

America handicaps disabled people. And because that is true, we are handicapping America itself.

This book is about what we are doing and how we are doing it, about the barriers people themselves erect and can eliminate, about the attitudes and creations that handicap America by handicapping disabled people. Only when we have seen the problems can we see the solutions. Only then can we begin to build a barrier-free America, just as we have constructed a barrier-filled society.

Almost 36 million Americans have physical, mental, and emotional disabilities. One out of six—one of the largest minorities in America today. We must come to see that these people we call "disabled" are also people with abilities, individuals who have important contributions to make in our society, but who face obstacles all of us have wittingly and unwittingly set in their paths.

We must see that each of us—salespeople, merchants, bankers, architects, writers, lawyers, doctors, policemen, administrators, social workers, nurses, students, teachers, therapists, advertisers, disabled people themselves and their employers, co-workers, families, friends, and neighbors—has played and plays a role, however small, in creating these obstacles, and that each of us can contribute to their removal. The slow and continuing accretion of barriers can be halted, and then the process can be reversed. All of us daily build today's America and all of us can help to build a new America.

We need to see what costs we incur because of these barriers: the economic costs, which run into the billions annually, and more important, the staggering human and moral costs of depriving people of an opportunity to earn a living and live a life.

We need to understand that this is one minority that respects no age, race, sex, or class privileges. Anyone can become disabled. A skiing accident, a highway collision, a mistaken dose of medicine—it may take seconds or it may take years. The obstacles that confront disabled people today may face all of us someday. A mother pushing a carriage experiences some of these barriers. So, too, does a temporarily disabled businessman. The barriers that hamper 36 million Americans today are important because they deprive our country of badly needed manpower, deplete our national resources, waste human lives, cheapen the quality of life in our country, and potentially affect all of us, man, woman, and child.

For two hundred years, we have designed a nation for the average, normal, able-bodied majority, little realizing that millions cannot enter many of our buildings, ride our subways and buses, enjoy our educational and recreational programs and facilities, and use our communications systems. We have created an image of disabled people that is perhaps the greatest barrier they face. We see the disability—the chrome and the leather, the guide dog, the hearing aid, the crutches—and look the other way. Just as we cannot seem to see the man in the policeman, so imposing are the uniform and the cultural expectations that go with it, so we cannot see the woman in the wheelchair. We do not see, nor do we look to find, her abilities, interests, and desires. We condescend, we mutter hurried excuses, and we flee—because we do not understand, and somewhere inside us, we are afraid to understand.

There are in this country tens of millions of people who have dificulty hearing, seeing, moving, learning, controlling their emotions, talking. But all are people. Their disabilities are real, but so are their abilities. They are disabled, but they need not be handicapped.

Yet we handicap them.

We smile at a poster child and hope for her, but when she wants to go to school we do not let her attend ours and when she grows up we do not want to know her. When disabled adults apply for jobs for which they are qualified we look for ways to deny them employment. When they seek housing we suggest they look somewhere else. And we are very persuasive, because our homes, buildings, and communities are often inaccessible to wheelchairs, feature communications systems deaf people cannot use, and have safety warnings blind people cannot read. Yet we do more: almost each new day brings to light cases of disabled people being vandalized, discriminated against, raped, denied permission to marry, fired, institutionalized, deprived of their children, sent to out-of-the-way "special" programs, robbed, and even killed.

We have said for two hundred years, and say anew

each day, that we do not wish to see disabled people and disabilities. We do not want to be reminded of their needs or burdened with their desires to live in the world. If America handicaps disabled people, it is because we have made it so. We prefer these people to be sequestered safely in secluded institutions—and they have been. We prefer them to remain second-class citizens—and they are. We prefer them to be invisible—and they strive, many of them, to be so, in hopes of perhaps that way finally gaining our acceptance.

Most of all, we stubbornly refuse to acknowledge that the problems disabled people face are not theirs alone. We label these people and categorize them apart from the rest of us, somehow more different than like us, not deserving of the opportunities we take for granted. When someone close to us becomes disabled, our immediate reaction is to hide the disability out of shame, embarrassment, and, often, guilt. We should not be surprised when many disabled people come to see themselves as we see them, retreating from social interaction, hiding, desperately attempting to "pass" as normal. The vicious circle produces a hidden minority, impotent, hesitant—and contributing less and less to America.

Disabled people have been out of the mainstream of American life for two hundred years. And these years have seen the construction of modern American society —its values, its heritage, its cities, its transportation and communications networks. So that now, when they are coming back into our society, the barriers they face are enormous. Today, disabled people seek very basic rights. They want a place to live—and cannot find it. They want an education—and are turned away. They seek access to transportation on buses and subways—and cannot get on. They desire the right to vote—but cannot get in. They want entertainment—but cannot enjoy it. They seek jobs—and are rejected. They desire respect —and receive humiliation.

Almost every American knows someone who is disabled, is himself or herself disabled in some way, or will eventually become disabled. In fact, the day will come when there will be one chronically ill, elderly, or disabled American for every able-bodied citizen. Because we deny this, because we look the other way, because we hide disabilities and disabled people, we hasten that day. And we erect yet more barriers to disabled people, constructing daily a society that becomes ever more oppressive to disabled individuals—and to America itself.

We do not see this vast minority. Or perhaps we do not see because we will not look. It is painful for many of us to see disabilities and difficult to see beyond them to abilities. So we deny, we hide, we forget.

We are making a mistake.

This book is about that mistake. But more, it is about people. People who daily step over curbs, watch TV, climb imposing stairways, listen to the radio, vote, ride escalators, drink from water fountains—and people who cannot do these things; people who design and construct buildings and subways, programs and facilities—and people who cannot use them. It is about people who command respect and people who could, but rarely do. It is about people in America today, people who strive to ascend higher than their dreams and people who strive just to make it through the day.

These pages chronicle handicapping conditions of our

own creation, obstacles we have created that hamper the flight of a man's spirit. For at the instant Neil Armstrong uttered the historic words: "That's one small step for man, one giant leap for mankind," there were in Houston and New York and the rest of America tens of millions of disabled people whose onerous environments forced them to take small steps, to exhaust themselves in mundane tasks that left little time for ascending to the heights of which they were capable and the creativity to which they aspired.

There were then and are today architectural, attitudinal, educational, occupational, legal, and personal barriers constraining the spirits and bodies of millions of American people. For one six-inch curb can stop a man. So, too, can the daily degradations of passers-by and salespeople, persistent poverty, inferior and often segregated schooling, archaic and meaningless laws, long-term joblessness, damaged self-concepts, and restricted interaction with other people. These barriers, these environments, impose limitations and exact penalties often far greater than do the disabilities themselves.

When the effort merely to get out of the house or to understand the words of another human being is so great that it commands every available ounce of energy, a man's spirit can rarely soar. But when a person overcomes these barriers through a conscious act of will, only to face obstacles other people have wittingly or unwittingly placed in his or her path, when he or she cannot locate a home or command the respect of associates, the spirit may die. If so, the spirit of each of us dies a little with it.

That in the last quarter of the twentieth century so

many Americans are without usable housing, transportation, and medical care; that millions must struggle through each and every day just to survive, with precious little opportunity to live; that today so many must battle daily to maintain some semblance of self-respect: all of this can only be considered an outrage.

The problems disabled people face are not theirs alone but confront all of us, and all of us can help to remove them. I have written this book for the people who can help overcome the barriers America has placed in the paths of its disabled citizens, and so open up new vistas of creativity and productiveness in our nation. I have tried to focus attention upon the questions as I see them and to propose what I believe may prove effective answers.

For America need not be handicapping nor need it be handicapped. Because each of us is part of the problem, each can become part of the solution. People have erected these barriers, and people can eliminate them. The barriers we have constructed for two hundred years will not disappear in two. But an America that can make giant leaps can surely take small steps.

A book is the work of many hands. Of all those who lent theirs to help me with this one, I would like especially to thank Martin Sternberg, who helped me get started; my editor at Harper & Row, Harold Grove, who helped keep me going; Joseph Owens and Richard Melia, who proffered helpful comments, most of which I have adopted; and most of all, my wife, Phyllis, and daughter Doran who were always there when I needed them.

"Independence and self-confidence, the feeling
of creativity . . . , lives of high spirits rather
than hushed, suffocating silence."
—Supreme Court in *Papachriston
v. City of Jacksonville,* 405,
U.S. 156, 164 (1972)

"Rights are declared as absolutes, but they
ripple out into the world in an exceedingly
contingent fashion."
—S. Scheingold in *The Politics of Right.*

HANDICAPPING AMERICA

1

First Thoughts

The man who first walked on the barren crevasses of the moon was almost exactly like the man twenty thousand years ago who tended his mammoth herds by the light of that same moon, and who wondered at it. Both are the children of two million years of biological evolution: both are *Homo sapiens*. Yet one transcended his environment; the other adapted to it. One specialized narrowly, focusing his energies upon a single intensely creative activity that exploded the boundaries of knowledge; the other remained a generalist and a traditionalist, erecting his own stone and clay huts, hunting his own meat, making his own leather and skin clothes, chipping his own tools, living and reliving an endless succession of virtually identical days. One could not even begin to teach his father all he had learned and himself fathered children who will barely recognize the problems that filled his days, so different will be the tasks of their lives; the other repeated his father's work and procreated great-grandchildren who did precisely what he had done, having learned little that was new.

I choose to contrast these two men because I believe

that the environment a man faces determines the problems he will set himself to solve. Where the environment is harsh and forbidding, a man will concentrate every fiber upon survival. As time evolves, he will remove one barrier after another, freeing himself to turn to the next. And this is what is so majestic about man: that by conquering his environment he frees his mind.

The environments disabled Americans face today are in many respects more forbidding than those early man confronted in equatorial Africa. Prehistoric man could at least ensure his own survival, design his accommodations to meet his needs, and learn what he had to know. He was master of his own fate more than are many disabled people in twentieth-century America who face barriers to simple needs and rights, to housing, transportation, and the means to make a living for themselves.

Small Steps

We usually consider ourselves humane and enlightened in our "management" of disabilities compared with earlier generations. And we are. But the analogy is not really a fair one: the historical antecedents of our current attitudes toward and programs for disabled people defy that neat a dichotomy.

Man emerged in equatorial Africa about one million years ago. The archaeological digs in China and Germany and the Middle East are pregnant with suggestive data about *Homo erectus,* Neanderthal man, and, later, *Homo sapiens.* Earliest man was almost certainly a hunter and a forager, a tool maker and user. He did not live long, twenty years perhaps, and every day of those twenty years he depended for his very survival upon other men. For man was slow, awkward, and relatively defenseless. His hunt was a communal activity, a small group of men surrounding the prey and closing in.

Each man was vital to the hunt, and to the continued existence of the group. The day afforded literally no time for any man who could not contribute his share of the work. But there was another, equally compelling, factor in this: earliest man was a nomad, forever on the move. A carnivore must follow the prey, and when one flock is depleted, another must be found. Those who could not follow were left behind to die.

This was not the callous indifference it may seem. Early man had no alternative. A person who could not see, or hear, or walk was a liability to the entire group: a daily threat to its very existence. And so disabled children were left to die, or killed, perhaps with little compunction. Many died on their own, made more vulnerable to disease and to the elements by their disabilities.

There is evidence that prehistoric man practiced trephining—cutting holes in the skull to enable evil spirits to escape. This suggests that early man had some kind of demonological conception of the nature of human personality. The existence of an immaterial animus, or power, that could control a person's behavior provided a ready explanation for personality disorders, mental illness, and perhaps other disabilities as well.

The concept that handicaps result from interactions between disabilities and environments is well illustrated in primitive culture. Survival there depends upon strength, agility, and sensory acuity, so physical disabilities become handicapping. But intellectual superiority, the ability to calculate and to read, artistic creativity, and certain other aspects of exceptionality are of little survival value in a primitive culture. Consequently, brilliant and highly talented infants and children who had physical defects and similarly endowed youths who became disabled may have been killed or left to die while mildly and moderately retarded children were kept alive because their disabilities were less handicapping.

A group on the move cannot create a civilization. Early man carried with him only what was absolutely essential. It would be pointless to build when the stay would be a short one. And it would be equally pointless to remain behind to care for the infirm when food is no longer available.

It was not until man became a gardener, as the valleys of the Euphrates and the Tigris began to support vegetation, that any kind of civilization emerged. Twenty thousand years ago man attached himself to a herd, following it wherever it went. Sometime during the next ten thousand years he began to domesticate some animals and to tend to some plants. This was the agricultural revolution that produced settled villages and, eventually, civilization.

In the great arc of the Fertile Crescent, and again in the New World, women harvested wheat and maize equally with men. And clay was molded into bricks, which in turn became buildings. With the change from nomadic to agricultural life-styles, man settled down. Now he invented tools—the pot, the needle, the sickle, the nail, and, in the Old World but not in the New, the wheel. There was now a little medicine, shelter, and, this is important, time. For when constant movement ceased to drive a tribe, there was time to care for the weak and the disabled. And with less need for moving and hunting, strength, ability, and sensory acuity became less important. Disabled persons could contribute to the life of a village, in a limited way perhaps, but at least they were no longer a total liability. They could plant and harvest food, sew, construct tools, make pottery, be more independent and self-sufficient than they could have been in earlier times.

Yet the belief persisted that disabilities were somehow supernaturally inspired, that some sinister, demonological force permeated the air, striking a mind here, a spirit there, twisting a body or destroying a sense. Disabilities were feared precisely because they were not understood. Prehistoric man needed some explanations for the phenomena he experienced, and those he could not comprehend he attributed to unknown forces. Gradually, over thousands of years, man found that his world was in fact predictable—that the movements of the sun and the stars followed certain patterns, that clouds meant possible rain, that lightning and fire were somehow akin, and that plants would grow under certain conditions and could be harvested at predictable times.

And then a remarkable thing happened: man began to look at man as he had learned to look at nature. This is exciting precisely because it is so difficult for man to question the obvious, to see the commonplace clearly, and to ask elegantly simple questions. And what is more evident than man's very existence and behavior itself? Yet it was thousands of years after man had questioned the seasons and begun to understand their regularity that he started to question himself in search of similar regularities. The work of the Greek philosophers Anaxagoras and Diogenes, and later Aristotle, led to the concept of mind, or *nous* as it was called, as central to man's understanding of man. Aristotle, in particular, saw man as a natural phenomenon, with mind and body analogous to function and structure.

Disabilities were common in Aristotle's day, with warriors frequent victims of debilitating injuries and plagues rampant, with infant mortality and morbidity rates extremely high. To his contemporaries, disabilities were visible, an everyday part of life, too common to excite much comment. It remained for Aristotle and those who followed him to question disabilities, their causes, their effects upon people, and what might be done about them. Again, the question was the difficult step, but once it had been asked, an answer would eventually follow.

Aristotle looked at deaf people and said they did not learn because human intercourse through speech was central to education. Hippocrates and Galen, the founders of modern medicine, looked at epilepsy and said it was a disturbance of natural processes in the mind. What is important is not their answers—Aristotle, for example, concluded that deaf people were uneducable—but their questions. They asked simple questions and sought simple, natural answers. The questions represented the beginning of a quantum leap forward in treatment of disabled people.

But the leap was a long time in completion. Aristotle's ideas had not yet generated much influence upon general thinking when the Christian era began. The example set by Jesus of seeking out and helping disabled people inaugurated a new period of sympathy and pity toward persons with disabilities. Church men and women began to organize services for disabled persons, doing much that was needed but also creating a provider-receiver relationship that continues to this day to characterize charitable causes. By supplying food and shelter, religious groups assumed a position as providers, a position of superiority and control. The price was a stiff one for the receiver—dislocation, often, and subservience to the provider, a subservience that carried with it a loss of autonomy and self-determination.

Underlying the new charity was a conviction that Christian theology justified these actions on the grounds that disability was an indication of impurity and evidence of a soul that needed to be saved. The question of whether a man was helped when control of his destiny was removed from his hands appeared little to concern the early Christians in their zeal to perform good works.

Then, as now, a great deal depended upon who it was who became disabled. Firstborn sons of wealthy landlords received special attention and services denied to less fortunate individuals. In the Far East another pattern emerged. Upper-class Chinese and Tibetan individuals might deliberately disable themselves and their offspring as a dramatic demonstration of their ability to have someone else do their work for them—by, for example, keeping their fists clenched until fingernails grew into the palms. At the other end of the social-class continuum, beggars might cripple their children to generate greater sympathy for their appeals.

The thousand years of the Middle Ages further delayed the leap Aristotle had begun. Supernaturalism returned in full force. Disabled people were to be feared or ridiculed, objects of persecution on the one hand and court jesters on the other. It was not until the Renaissance that Paracelsus, among others, began to recommend medical treatment and that schools were established for disabled children and youths. Again, it was the wealthy heirs whose disabilities spurred special-education programs. Firstborn sons who were deaf, for example, could not inherit estates unless they could read and write. Tutoring provided for them soon produced special-education programs for other disabled children as well. In Spain, Ponce de León demonstrated that deaf people could be taught (that Aristotle was wrong). Mentally retarded children began receiving custodial and, in some cases, educational services. The differences between various disabilities came to be more widely recognized and began to produce differences in education and in care.

But Aristotle's leap was not yet complete. People on both sides of the Atlantic still feared disabilities and sought to remove them from sight. In Germany and in France a gradual emergence of disabled individuals from the seclusion of their homes began late in the eighteenth century. England, too, gingerly at first, inaugurated some services in the community for children and adults who were disabled.

In America, progress was slow. The earliest colonists had emigrated from deteriorating cities in Europe where unwanted dependents had become burdens of the public treasury. Quite naturally, the colonies desired to restrict immigration of individuals, including those who were physically or mentally disabled, who might become dependents needing financial support. Settlement laws were enacted requiring an individual to live and work for a period of three months to one year before legal residence could be established; those who could not support themselves were asked to leave unless a resident of good financial standing agreed to assume responsibility for their care.

Community mores stressed self-sufficiency and independence. Indolence was seen as the principal source of poverty. Disabled individuals rarely were believed capable of achieving financial self-support; the concept of education and rehabilitation to overcome the disability was largely unknown. Rather, existence of a disability appeared reason enough to deny a person the opportunity to participate in community life. Because the family formed the central social unit, providing education, food, and other material goods today supplied by political and economic institutions, disabled children and adults were expected to remain at home, cared for by their families.

Gradually, as the population increased, pressure for institutionalization of disabled individuals increased. Almshouses providing food and shelter were established late in the seventeenth century to serve able-bodied poor and disabled persons whose families could not or would not support them. But it was not until the middle of the eighteenth century that medical and educational services became available. The first school for deaf children was established in Hartford, Connecticut, in 1817; by 1880 most of the states had institutional-education programs for deaf, blind, and mentally retarded individuals. Humanitarian reasons provided only one impetus; more urgent was pervasive fear of "lunatics" and "afflicted" persons whom the community desired to remove from the streets.

Material plenty inspired a belief that social ills soon would be eradicated and a parallel conviction that lack of personal success must be attributable to unworthiness and laziness. These ideals, fostered by the frontier movement, worked against the formulation of a social policy of public assistance to needy individuals. But the prevailing hope for a better world focused attention upon any existing deficiencies. Together, these forces led to a gradual and halting emergence of services for disabled individuals. Thus, able-bodied persons were moved out of almshouses and sent to special workplaces to earn their own keep while disabled persons remained behind; only gradually did the concept evolve that the latter had abilities that could be socially useful and that should be tapped by work programs. Even where disabled persons performed some work, they seldom left the institution for any reason. For institutions performed a valuable function: they kept disabilities out of sight and out of mind so that the public sensibility would not be offended.

Almshouses and other institutions were characterized by an appalling lack of sanitary conditions and attentive care. Just as the residents were sheltered from public view, so too were the conditions in which they were herded together—old and young, epileptic and retarded, sane and insane, criminal and juvenile delinquent—in physically degrading settings. It remained for Dorothea Dix and those who followed her to expose these conditions and force improvements. Miss Dix succeeded in persuading the Congress to pass a law in 1854 to finance mental hospitals with federal funds. President Franklin Pierce, influenced by prevailing notions of limited federal powers, vetoed the bill. His decision established a powerful precedent that severely restricted efforts to improve institutional care for the next half century. Returning to the state level, Miss Dix succeeded in founding more than twenty mental hospitals and in enlarging others.

In Boston, Dr. Samuel Gridley Howe established the Massachusetts Asylum for the Blind (now the Perkins Institute) in 1832 and began educational services designed to provide blind children and youths with the same kind of experiences public schools were offering to able-bodied children. Together with the American Asylum for the Deaf and Dumb (now the American School for the Deaf) in Hartford, Connecticut, the Boston school inaugurated a new era in American attitudes toward disabled people. In these schools deaf and blind children were shown to be capable of learning and of putting to good use their knowledge and skills. The American Asylum had employed Laurent Clerc, a deaf Frenchman, as a teacher, establishing another revolutionary precedent. Massachusetts served as the site for the first programs educating mentally retarded individuals. Progress with these persons was less dramatic than with deaf and blind children, however, as unrealistic hopes of curing retardation gave way to a cautious optimism that these people could learn limited skills and acquire the ability to care for at least some of their needs. It was not until the end of the nineteenth century that programs for orthopedically disabled persons were started, largely because medical knowledge and particularly the science of orthopedics developed slowly. Clifford Beers's autobiography, *A Mind That Found Itself* (1908) was enormously influential in helping to inaugurate services for mentally ill individuals.

As in prior wars, servicemen returning from World War I who had incurred service-connected disabilities encountered severe adjustment problems at home. While previously, compensation to disabled veterans of American wars had been limited to government pensions, the large number of soldiers disabled during the 1914–1918 conflict, combined with increasing societal concern for disabled people in general, led to the enactment on June 27, 1918, of the Smith-Sears Vocational Rehabilitation Act appropriating federal funds for job training and education for disabled veterans. The act is significant because it represents a major advance beyond institutionalization and beyond education on the elementary and secondary level to encompass vocational preparation and job placement of disabled persons.

Equally significant was the action on the home front during the war. Because large numbers of workers were drafted into the armed forces, disabled adults were able to secure jobs in unprecedented numbers and to demonstrate their abilities to work. In 1920, largely as a result of positive wartime experiences of industry with disabled workers, the Congress passed a Vocational Rehabilitation Act for civilians who were disabled. The act inaugurated a state-federal partnership in which federal financial assistance was offered on a matching basis to state agencies which provided counseling, training, and job placement services. The program focused from its beginning upon the less severely disabled population; blind persons, for example, were usually excluded.

The ascendance of Franklin Delano Roosevelt to the presidency in 1932, eleven years after his legs had been paralyzed by poliomyelitis, marked the beginning of a major change in America's treatment of its disabled citizens. Roosevelt was severely disabled yet that is not what the American public saw. Instead, it witnessed an able, confident, assertive, and, above all, active, individual leading the country into new and exciting prosperity. Three years after he first took office, Roosevelt signed the Social Security Act that established old-age and survivors' benefits, unemployment compensation, and programs for disabled children and adults. The act represented a recognition that assistance to disabled persons was a matter of social justice, not charity. James Thurber, who was long blind in one eye and later became blind in the other; Al Capp, who had lost his left leg at the age of nine; and Glenn Cunningham, who overcame a childhood accident that left him severely physically disabled to become the "world's fastest human" illustrated for the public the potentials of disabled individuals. The Vocational Rehabilitation Act of 1943 (the Barden-LaFollette Act) enlarged the federal-state "VR" program, including for the first time physical and mental restoration services and establishing an Office of Vocational Rehabilitation separate from the Office of Education in the Federal Security Agency (now the Department of Health, Education, and Welfare). The 1954 Vocational Rehabilitation Amendments added research and professional training authorizations to the program.

From 1950 to 1969 one woman exerted more influence in upgrading the quality of life in America for disabled persons than anyone else in public life. Mary E. Switzer was administrator of the vocational rehabilitation program, first as commissioner of the Office of Vocational Rehabilitation and later as Administrator of the Social and Rehabilitation Service, both in HEW. The highest-ranking woman in federal career civil service in her time, she presided over and guided the expansion of services for disabled adults that has successfully assisted tens of thousands of individuals achieve self-sufficiency and independence despite severe disabilities. During her administration, the rehabilitation budget rose from $20.5 million to over $500 million; more significantly, she broadened the agency's work in highly creative and productive directions—supporting, for example, the National Theater of the Deaf—which enhanced the cultural life of the nation while providing satisfying careers for disabled persons.

During the 1960s, the powerful social turbulence unleashed by demands of black Americans for equality of opportunity in education, employment, and community life led to expanded programming for disabled people, especially for mentally retarded individuals, who were singled out for attention by the Kennedy and Johnson administrations. Organizations of and for disabled people assumed unprecedented importance in the determination of social policy toward disabled individuals. The American Foundation for the Blind had been enormously influential for decades, but it was not until the mid-1960s that consumer groups such as the National Association of the Deaf and the Paralyzed Veterans of America began to assert the right of disabled people to speak for themselves.

The early 1970s began with retrenchment in the face of severe economic crises that led to widespread unemployment among able-bodied as well as disabled persons. Far stronger programs for women and minority-group members than were in existence for disabled persons produced a tendency by industry to employ females and members of racial minorities rather than disabled persons for the few available positions. A series of landmark legislative victories for disabled persons in mid-decade began what will probably lead to historic advances. The Rehabilitation Act of 1973, which contains the best civil rights protection provisions ever enacted on behalf of disabled individuals; the Education for All Handicapped Children Act of 1975, which requires a free and appropriate public education for all disabled children and youth; and the Developmentally Disabled Assistance and Bill of Rights Act of 1975, which coordinates services for retarded, cerebral palsied, autistic, and epileptic individuals, are historic in the protection they offer for disabled persons. A number of court decisions mandating equal educational opportunities for disabled children and youth produced a nationwide movement toward "mainstreaming" in which disabled children attend the same schools and the same classrooms as do able-bodied children. The new laws and court decisions may mark the beginning of a new era, with disabled persons coming into the mainstream of American life after two centuries of exclusion. The implementation of these laws and court decisions, however, has yet to fulfill the promise they contain.

It is clear, however, that throughout the centuries treatment of disabled people has been inadequate not so much because of evil intent by able-bodied individuals—although there *has* been that—as because of harsh environmental pressures on entire societies, public attitudes reflecting ignorance and fear of disabilities, public and private programs designed to benefit other groups which often had unexpected side effects on disabled peo-

ple themselves. For it is only within the past decade that
public and private officials have begun to look to disabled
people for input on decisions to any significant extent
and only within the past five years that disabled adults
have systematically demanded that input.

As America enters its third century, disabled citizens
are at last obtaining the opportunity to plead their own
causes. How successfully they do so, and how effectively
they join their causes with those of other minority groups
and of the country itself, will largely determine how
America will treat disabled people in the decades to
come.

Who Is Disabled?

When we talk about disability, our first question is: Disabled for what? We begin with an impairment, which results from disease, accident, or a defective gene. If the
impairment persists for six months or longer and interferes with a person's ability to do something—walk, see,
hear, talk, dress, learn, lift, go to school, work—we say
the person has a disability. When a disability, in interaction with a specific set of environmental conditions,
makes an individual unable to perform certain activities,
we say he or she is handicapped. Yet, and this is important, it would be more appropriate to say that the environment itself is handicapping. A blind person is handicapped with respect to watching a Charlie Chaplin film,
for example, but not while listening to a radio broadcast;
the reverse is true for a deaf person. We can remove the
handicaps by providing a soundtrack for the movie and a
printed script for the radio show. The individuals are still

disabled but they are no longer handicapped, at least not in these activities.

How many people are disabled? If we accept the definition proposed in 1966 by the Social Security Administration Survey of Disabled Adults—individuals aged 18 to 64 in the noninstitutionalized population who are limited in the kind or amount of work or housework they can do because of a chronic health condition or impairment lasting six months or longer—we arrive at a figure of 23.3 million disabled adults, according to the Urban Institute, which computed the figure in 1975 for the Rehabilitation Services Administration. This is 18.7 percent of the total U.S. noninstitutionalized population in that age range, or almost one in five. An additional 2 million Americans of all ages are disabled and living in institutions. According to the U.S. Office of Education and testimony presented in 1975 before the Senate Subcommittee on the Handicapped of the Committee on Labor and Public Welfare (now the Committee on Human Resources), there are another 8 million children and youth aged 3 to 21 who are sufficiently disabled to require special educational provisions in the public schools. And nearly one-quarter of America's 20 million elderly citizens are believed to be disabled. Allowing for the overlaps in these categorical estimates, we arrive at a figure of 36 million disabled Americans, which is the most widely quoted estimate. That it is an estimate is important. Few areas of American life are as little studied as is the demography of disability. The true number may be as low as 14 million or as high as 50 million.

Most disabled people were once able-bodied. Only about one in every six was born with a disability; the other five became disabled in childhood, adulthood, or old age. Improved medical care, ironically, is largely responsible for the fact that the number of disabled people is constantly rising. Infant mortality rates decline at the cost of ever higher disability rates in newborns. Twenty-five years ago, victims of severe spinal cord injury rarely lived more than six months after the onset of the disability; today, severe spinal cord injuries of more than ten years' duration are not uncommon. At the same time, modern medicine is increasing life expectancy dramatically. In 1900 the average life expectancy was 47 years; today it is 71 years. Ten percent of the American population is over 65 years of age. Many of these people cannot see as well as they once did, hear as well, lift their hands or feet as high, but they are alive. By 1985 the number of disabled Americans will increase by about 20 percent. By the year 2000 there will be one physically disabled, chronically ill, or over-65 person for every able-bodied individual. And, unless we drastically alter our current policies toward these people, half of America will be supporting the other half.

Six Barriers

As might be expected with a group as large as the 36 million disabled Americans, needs, desires, and problems vary widely. There are, nonetheless, some central issues common to the group as a whole. These issues concern barriers that are architectural, attitudinal, educational, occupational, legal, and personal in nature.

Architectural Barriers

That 36 million Americans are disabled and that the population of disabled Americans is increasing reinforces the necessity to design for all Americans, whether we are building an apartment complex, a bus, or a program. Yet when the Senate Special Committee on Aging held hearings on architectural design in October of 1971, testimony revealed that only one community, Owen Brown Village of Columbia, Maryland, then under construction, was designed to be totally barrier-free. When Timothy Nugent of the University of Illinois, one of the nation's premier experts on barrier-free design, confronted thirty-five architectural groups with figures showing that doorways to bathrooms and other parts of residential buildings typically were inaccessible to many nonambulatory disabled people, none of the architects could explain why the buildings had been designed that way, except to say that this was how it had always been done.

When Karoly Nagy of Middlesex (N.J.) County College investigated the accessibility of New Jersey state, county, and municipal buildings, he wondered how nonambulatory disabled citizens using wheelchairs and canes were supposed to present their cases at the seats of government, something the U.S. Supreme Court has said they have a right to do. Nagy found that the Woodbridge (N.J.) Municipal Building had 23 steps leading to its front door, New Brunswick's City Hall had 17 to its first floor, and Edison's City Hall had 7. Assuming a citizen in a wheelchair somehow got into the building, he or she would face 23 more steps in Woodbridge, 23 in New

Brunswick, and 19 in Edison before entering the mayor's office—all in buildings without elevators.

Looking at New Brunswick's schools, Nagy counted 16 steps to the first floor of Roosevelt Intermediate School and 24 steps between its four floors, 22 steps to the front door of A. Chester Redshaw School and 24 between its three floors, and 18 steps between the first and second floors of New Brunswick High School—all without elevators.

In 1965 the U.S. Senate voted funds for the construction of the Washington, D.C., METRO rapid transportation system and stipulated that the builders accommodate disabled and elderly citizens who presented special transportation needs. Despite the clear intent of Congress, the METRO planners first claimed that no funds were available to study the issues. When E. H. (Ted) Noakes, a nationally prominent architect, did an analysis under the auspices of the President's Committee on Employment of the Handicapped, his findings were ignored. Congress passed another law specifically mandating accessibility, including the use of elevators where necessary to accommodate passengers who could not use stairs or escalators. Still, METRO refused to act. By this time, late in 1970, the federal commitment to METRO exceeded one billion dollars.

In 1972 Richard Heddinger, a statistician in the Bureau of Labor Statistics, and three interested organizations sued the builders. On October 23, 1973, Judge William B. Jones of the U.S. District Court for the District of Columbia issued an injunction halting any construction that would have to be removed or modified later to permit accessibility. Eighteen months later METRO officials were back in court asking that the injunction be lifted so the first three stations could be opened—one, Gallery Place, without elevators. In 1976, with much of the system already built, METRO belatedly permitted Gallaudet College, the world's only liberal arts college exclusively for deaf students, to conduct a study of transportation barriers hearing-impaired persons might face in using the subway—eleven years and hundreds of millions of dollars after the recommendations of such a study might have been implemented at little or no cost. On August 31, 1976, Judge Jones refused yet another METRO request to lift the injunction. Gallery Place finally got an elevator in July, 1977—twelve years after Congress first ordered accessibility.

The case represents the first known instance in American history that a public facility's opening was delayed because it was not accessible to disabled people. And it is important also because it reflects the forces and counterforces at play in America today on the issue of accessibility. Why did METRO resist congressional orders? Why did it take five years of court pressure to bring an elevator to Gallery Place? Whatever the answers, the long resistance of METRO officials is hardly unique. Barrierfree design is a hotly contested battleground in this country today and is likely to continue to be controversial for years to come.

The issues concern more than stairs and escalators. Doors must be at least 30 inches wide for wheelchair accessibility, but almost all doors in this country are narrower than 24 inches and many are revolving or otherwise inaccessible. Blind persons cannot read printed signs or directions, yet raised letters would be easily un-

derstood. Deaf persons cannot hear spoken announcements or auditory-based warning signals, but printed instructions and lights would be accessible to them. Elevator
buttons typically are placed above the reach of people in
wheelchairs; many of the buttons are activated not by
pressure but by the heat of a finger, frustrating wheelchair users who try to reach the button with metal instruments. Ramps enabling people in wheelchairs to cir-
cumvent stairs are often sloped steeply, presenting
dangerous obstacles, while inclined ramps may provide
no resting spots for wheelchairs.

Attitudinal Barriers

Dartmouth psychologist Robert Kleck has spent eleven
years investigating attitudes toward disability. He has
found that able-bodied people generally express neutral-
to-positive feelings toward disabled individuals. Physiological readings, however, such as eye-movement patterns, sweat, heart rate, and other indices reveal high
anxiety, avoidance of the disabled person's eyes, and rejection of his or her presence. Overt rejection is socially
unacceptable, so able-bodied people smile at disabled persons and voice agreement with opinions they do not hold
for fear of offending the disabled individual or being
thought heartless. Kleck's work is important because it
suggests that a falseness may pervade interactions between disabled and nondisabled people which may negatively affect the well-being of disabled individuals by misleading them as to their acceptability and producing
confused self-images. He is now investigating ways of improving these interactions so that both parties will feel

more comfortable and will be more honest with each other.

John Tringo of the University of Kentucky asked more than 450 students and rehabilitation workers to rank 21 disabilities from most to least acceptable. He was somewhat surprised to learn that severity of the disability had less to do with the rankings than did visibility. Those disabilities that were most visible were among the least tolerable while those that were less visible were more acceptable. Visibility is closely related to understanding: it seems that nondisabled people fear most those disabilities they do not understand and which are consequently potentially threatening.

Our attitudes toward disabilities seem to be a curious amalgam of fear and ignorance, optimism and loathing. We know, most of us, that we will eventually become disabled (if we live long or dangerously enough), yet we take out astonishingly little disability insurance. We applaud stories about overachieving "super-cripples," yet segregate disabled children in basement classrooms and isolated institutions. We admire Christy Brown's literary efforts (*Down All the Days, My Left Foot,* etc.), yet wonder at his exuberant embrace of life when the only part of his body he can move voluntarily is his left foot. We don't understand, and sometimes it seems we don't want to.

Our national leaders reflect our ignorance and confusion. When, in April, 1976, the American Coalition of Citizens with Disabilities (ACCD), a nationwide organization representing disabled people, requested policy statements on disability from the eight men who were at the time contenders for presidential nominations, not one appeared in person. Five did send representatives to the

ACCD conference. The spokesmen had no comprehensive policies to present, however, and their speeches revealed such ignorance that the audience could only stare in disbelief (one, for example, spoke only of certification for institutions). The Department of Housing and Urban Development persisted for years in combining housing programs for elderly and disabled people, despite the protestations of both groups that their needs and desires differ greatly. HUD sponsored mammoth, multi-million-dollar public housing projects few disabled people want to live in rather than supporting architectural accessibility in all residential facilities, which most disabled people favor. The Tax Reform Act of 1976 required Social Security disability insurance recipients to pay taxes on their payments: the confusing statute, since repealed, meant that most persons receiving disability or sick pay were to pay federal taxes on the entire amount, retroactive to January 1, 1976. The vast majority of federal funds spent on programs serving disabled people goes not to helping them help themselves through training and job placement but to income maintenance programs that actually discourage disabled people from seeking work.

Attitudinal barriers are particularly critical because attitudes influence and underlie actions. Teachers will not exert much effort on or require much performance from students they do not believe can achieve, nor will employers hire applicants they do not believe can do the job. In America today disabled people are defined by their disabilities, not by their abilities, and public policy reflects these attitudes.

Educational Barriers

Of the estimated 8 million disabled children and youth, one million are out of school altogether. Current figures indicate that only 3.9 million of the 8 million, or fewer than half, are receiving an appropriate education. The quality of special-education programming provided to this minority has been a source of long-standing concern to parents, educators, and disabled people alike.

The overall focus of special education is more on the disabilities than on the abilities of the children. Teacher-training programs, for example, provide extensive instruction to prospective teachers on the anatomy and physiology of particular disabilities but little by comparison on their unimpaired abilities. In the field of education for deaf children, to take one instance, the program of instruction for teachers-in-training approved by the Bureau of Education for the Handicapped (which funds most of the programs) and required by the Council on Education of the Deaf (which certifies teachers) contains courses on the anatomy and physiology of the ear and of the speech mechanisms, but does not include courses on the eye, visual perception, nonverbal learning, or manual communication. The latter may be optional in some programs but to take them would normally mean the student must delay receiving his or her degree or take an unusually heavy load of courses. Analogously, schools for deaf children routinely include on their staffs audiologists and even otologists, but rarely optometrists or ophthalmologists. Extensive training is provided for the children in optimal use of whatever residual hearing they have, which is important, but far too little is done to teach the children to use their eyes effectively and efficiently, which is also important. The focus is not unique to deafness. Rather, it is a general problem. The stress is upon remediation of disability without a corresponding emphasis on development of abilities.

Even more basic is the entire question of segregation of children by their disabilities rather than by their abilities and interests. Educators have come to understand that removing disabled children from their community schools and classrooms may not be in their best interests and that the fact that two children share a disability does not mean they share abilities. Still, education of disabled children that focuses upon developing their strengths and preparing them for constructive lives and careers in the mainstream of American life remains more a goal than a reality.

When we turn to higher education, we find barriers equally as great. Undereducation on lower levels restricts the opportunities of disabled youth and adults to continue their education. Architectural and attitudinal barriers as imposing as those in other areas of American life confront disabled students in colleges and universities. A 1976 study by Abt Associates of Cambridge, Massachusetts, asked 3,038 colleges to cooperate in a survey of barriers to disabled students. One-third of the colleges agreed. By June 1, 1976, when the seven-month response period ended, only 500 had replied to the questionnaire. Of these, 120 had some special provisions to meet the needs of disabled students. The survey is as revealing of college and university programs for what it did not find as for what it did: only one-sixth of the colleges asked to participate completed the self-evaluation questionnaire, raising serious questions as to the scope and depth of the programs offered in higher education as a whole.

In 1971 a task force on higher education for disabled students declared that such students would encounter no particular problems attending California State University and College (CSUC) system campuses. David Travis, an assistant dean in the office of the CSUC chancellor didn't believe it. Two years after the task force report Travis toured 14 of the 19 campuses and found only one building that met state requirements for accessibility. Travis did not bother visiting the other five campuses because "they had nothing for disabled students. It was pointless even to go there."

Occupational Barriers

According to the 1970 Census study of disabled Americans aged 16 to 64 who were not in institutions, 42 percent of those disabled six months or longer were employed. The unemployment rate paralleled that of the general population, but almost 63 percent of the employed were at or near the poverty level and 41 percent had given up looking for jobs. The 1966 Social Security Administration Survey of Disabled Adults found that, although disabled people represented only one-sixth of the civilian noninstitutionalized population of working age, a major proportion of manpower waste may be attributed to involuntary nonparticipation in the labor force, unemployment, and underemployment among disabled individuals. About 25 percent of all persons not in the labor force and one-fourth of all unemployed individuals were disabled (the term "unemployed" refers to active job seekers, while those not in the labor force are not soliciting work). Fully 13 percent of all welfare recipients were disabled people.

Underemployment is a serious problem among disabled workers. When education—one index of potential, although far from a perfect one—and occupational status are correlated, the results indicate that disabled people are much more likely to have jobs beneath their abilities, if indeed they are employed, than are nondisabled individuals. A far greater proportion of disabled than nondisabled workers are in the secondary labor force where seasonal employment, part-time work, and minimum-wage levels produce more uncertainty than security and turnover rates are extraordinarily high.

Rehabilitation, specifically the federal-state vocational rehabilitation program managed by the Rehabilitation Services Administration, has contributed greatly to the alleviation of unemployment and underemployment among disabled adults. In fact, congressional oversight hearings consistently demonstrate that for every dollar expended in rehabilitation of disabled people, about nine dollars are returned to the government through taxes paid by the now-employed or upgraded individuals. Yet in a confusion of priorities, less than 2 percent of the $20 billion spent annually by 61 federal programs that serve disabled people is allocated to train them for employment. Most of the money goes to income maintenance.

Social Security and Medicare regulations actually discourage many disabled people from looking for work because their support payments and medical benefits often exceed their likely after-tax earnings—and are much more predictable. If a disabled person is successful in obtaining employment that pays more than $3,000 a year, his or her support is terminated. According to recent reports, a person with paraplegia, for example, would have to earn more than $12,000 annually just to be able to afford the medical benefits available through Social Security and Medicare. And the job would have to be a stable one, secure from abrupt and arbitrary termination, because if the job were lost, a two-year wait is required before the medical support resumes. Because few severely disabled individuals are able to obtain such well-paying and steady jobs, many prefer not to work.

Dale Rusk, who is legally blind, diabetic, and was the recipient two years ago of a kidney transplant, argues this point. "I simply can't afford to work," he told Tom Millstead. Rusk, who has a B.A. in business and economics, cites a law passed in 1973 extending Medicare benefits to those who have received Social Security disability payments for two years as the major obstacle. Eager to work—he is an almost full-time volunteer with the Kidney Foundation of the Midwest, in Minnesota—Rusk told Millstead: "There's just no incentive for persons in my position to take a chance on resuming employment. To take a job now would end the protection I'll be getting from Medicare and would deprive me of future Medicare benefits if an emergency or some new problem arose. And with my health problems, there's no way that a private insurance company would cover me. I've checked. And no way that an employer would include me in his group health insurance plan." The 1973 law Rusk cites specifies that Medicare benefits would normally terminate

upon employment and that if a former recipient had to
reapply for Medicare, another two-year delay would be
required.

Legal Barriers

The first United States Supreme Court ruling on the
rights of disabled people not subject to the criminal process came on June 26, 1975. Almost 2,500 decisions in
nearly two hundred years, yet *O'Connor* v. *Donaldson* represented the Court's initial case on the civil and legal
rights of disabled people. Frank Laski, an attorney affiliated with the Public Interest Law Center of Philadelphia, described the background against which the case
appeared in a 1976 article published in *American Rehabilitation:*

. . . 5 years ago, when Donaldson first sought relief in federal
court, no federal court had recognized the right of mentally ill
and retarded to be protected from harm in custodial environments. No federal court had faced the issue of employment
discrimination against qualified handicapped persons. No federal court had confronted the issue of systematic denial of use
of public transportation and buildings by physically handicapped and elderly citizens.

Why so little activity prior to 1971? One factor is certainly
the historical exclusion of disabled people from the mainstream of American life. Another is the relative quies-
cence of other groups, including women and minority-
group members, before the 1960s. The legal challenges
of the latter groups probably encouraged many disabled
persons to begin to stand up for their rights as well. But

related to these factors and extending beyond them, lawyers familiar with disability and experienced in technical aspects of the problems of disabled persons (architecture, engineering, institutionalization, etc.) are few and far between. One expert in the area has even remarked that half the cases decided against disabled people in the early 1970s could probably have been thrown out of court on the grounds that capable counsel was not provided.

Nor has legislation offered measurably better protection until very recently. The problem now is not that the laws don't exist. They do, and they cover access to public buildings, transportation, civil rights, housing, and education, among other areas. Rather the problem is that many of these laws are only symbolic: they are not adequately enforced.

As an example, take the case of affirmative action in employment of disabled persons. The Rehabilitation Act of 1973 (P. L. 93–112) requires federal contractors and subcontractors to recruit, hire, promote, and accommodate disabled people. The law, however, is much weaker than the executive orders on affirmative action for women and minority-group members. No quotas are suggested, no timetables provided, and most important, there has been next to nothing in the way of federal surveys to determine that companies are in fact complying with the law. The Department of Labor, which has responsibility for this segment of the law (Section 503), relies upon disabled people to complain of unfair treatment for its enforcement work. Yet, few disabled people know about the protection afforded them because the department has done too little to publicize the law and the regulations that govern it, and those few who do know about it often hesitate to complain because they doubt the federal government will stand behind them and the law. Available evidence appears in part to support these doubts. The department has assigned a total of 75 persons nationwide to the program and this figure includes secretarial as well as professional personnel. Even the first steps have not been taken: as of this writing, late in 1977, no one has collected a list of covered contractors or has defined the skills needed to perform jobs, or has conducted more than routine spot checks on employers. I am not aware of a single contractor whose funds have been withdrawn for violation of the law, nor do I know of more than a few hundred disabled individuals who have obtained jobs or promotions as a direct result of the law's enforcement. Only very recently has the department evidenced a greater commitment to protecting the rights of disabled applicants and jobholders, and this change appears largely a result of pressure from disabled consumers.

Section 503 offers but one example of legislative provisions that have proved much weaker than originally envisioned. The Architectural Barriers Act of 1968 (P. L. 90–480), which contained the first provisions for architectural accessibility ever promulgated in federal legislation, was virtually worthless. It was never enforced. Five years later Congress authorized the creation of an Architectural and Transportation Barriers Compliance Board to enforce its provisions. Even then, the administration refused to fund the board on the level that was required. Progress is being made, in accessibility and in other areas, but almost invariably through a process of revisions and patchwork additions to weak laws that suggests a reluc-

tance on the part of the legislative and executive branches
to act firmly and forcefully on behalf of disabled people.

The issues are political ones. Ours is a representative
government which assumes from the outset that citizens
will have their needs represented at the seats of government. For disabled people, however, the assumption is
largely erroneous. The same architectural barriers that
have kept disabled people out of New Brunswick's City
Hall also keep them out of numerous polling places and
congressmen's local offices. In Los Angeles it is illegal to
use an absentee ballot if you are able to travel to a polling
place, even if you are not able to get in to vote. Statutes in
almost all states contain sweeping provisions denying
mentally retarded individuals the right to vote, despite
the fact that we do not know the precise level of intelligence needed to make reasoned voting decisions. The
attitudes that make daily interactions of disabled people
with able-bodied individuals so difficult are as pervasive
in politicians as in salespeople. And the same ignorance
about the needs of disabled people that the American Coalition of Citizens with Disabilities found in presidential
candidates' representatives obtains in Senators, Congressmen, judges, and bureaucrats as well. Disabled people
often do not have the access needed to influence political
decisions and may not even be able to visit their representatives or vote in elections.

By contrast, businessmen who do not wish to spend
large amounts of money renovating buildings, educators
who do not wish to include disabled children in regular
school classrooms, employers who do not wish to hire
disabled adults, and almost every other segment of American society can summon much greater political influence.

When push comes to shove, disabled people are shown the (inaccessible) door. Very recently, there have been changes. Civil rights groups have begun to see that if anyone in America is denied basic protection, the rights of all are endangered. Elderly activists such as the American Association of Retired Persons and the Gray Panthers have begun to understand that many of their causes are also concerns of disabled people. Parents of disabled children are now working to improve the conditions their children will face as adults and are looking to disabled adults for assistance. Most important, disabled people are beginning to speak out for themselves. In Philadelphia a group of disabled adults sued the Department of Transportation for failing to comply with accessibility laws. In Berkeley disabled people have pushed through "blue curb laws," which require curb-cuts permitting wheelchairs access to streets and sidewalks. In New Orleans deaf people protested in a street demonstration when a musician was named superintendent of a school for deaf children. In Boston disabled adults placed city officials in wheelchairs, fitted them with tight-fitting plastic ear molds, and blindfolded them to increase their awareness of disabilities, and then followed up with specific legislative and administrative change proposals to improve services.

Personal Barriers

Most disabled people are adventitiously impaired. That is, they became disabled rather than being born that way. In 1974 the Kemper Insurance Group reported that the chances of a person's becoming disabled were relatively stable between the ages of 22 and 65, and were uniformly higher than the chances of dying in a given year. As people become disabled, they must not only adjust to the changed demands of everyday living but must also adapt to altered societal perceptions of them and their worth. A 1971 Social Security Administration survey of recently disabled adults revealed that these persons' incomes were more likely to have decreased than increased since the onset of the disability. As a combined result of the daily living problems emanating from the disability, reduced social status, and decreased income, recently disabled people frequently lower their perceptions of their own worth as human beings. Damaged self-concepts, in turn, lead to lowered aspirations and increased isolation, further handicapping the disabled individuals. A vicious circle is produced.

People disabled earlier in life face similar problems, but in addition receive what is almost always an inferior education and preparation for life, segregated from "normals" and sheltered from the harsh realities that await them as adults. The disabled adult, unlike the child, is required to meet or even exceed the levels of achievement set by able-bodied persons. The stress of moving from a sheltered environment into an oppressive and demanding one often causes high anxiety in disabled persons, frequently forcing them to be reclusive and to adopt protecting defense mechanisms. They tend to become highly sensitive to their impairments and attribute to them, as does the larger society, the root of many of their problems. As a consequence, hiding and/or denying the disability becomes an overriding concern.

Independent living, so basic and mundane for most of

us, is for many disabled people a challenging and sometimes unattainable goal. Martha Nelson, who died a few
years ago at the age of 103, spent 99 of those years in a
state mental hospital. At her death, state officials admit-
ted they did not know why she had been placed there or
why she had been retained for so long. John Gibson tells
of having to use the garbage ramp to get into a restau-
rant. In frustration at this and similar incidents, he
founded a group called WARPATH (World Association
to Remove Prejudice Against The Handicapped). Steve
Frazier was fired from his job with the Container Corporation of Renton, Washington, after he had a slight
seizure which caused no damage or injury. Judy Heu-
mann was arrested and removed from a National Airlines
jet because she was traveling unaccompanied and without
a medical certificate. Mervin Garretson switched brands
rather than fight because he kept getting cough syrup instead of the brand of cigarettes whose name he had difficulty pronouncing due to his hearing loss. Some of
these incidents may appear humorous, but to the people
experiencing them they are just a few of the humiliations
they endure daily in an insensitive America.

Sometimes the insensitivity threatens the lives of disabled people. Persons with disabilities are especially vulnerable to crime, because they present inviting targets to
muggers, rapists, vandals, and other criminals. Blind pe-
destrians cannot see their assailants, deaf shoppers cannot hear them, paraplegic individuals cannot flee, and cerebral palsied people involuntarily call attention to
themselves with their spasmodic movements. Many disabled persons are poor and live in low-income, high-crime
areas where help is slow to arrive. As the 1976 Demo-

cratic convention opened in Madison Square Garden, the New York *Post* juxtaposed a story on the Democratic platform call for a renewed assault on crime with an article from the AP wire about a 28-year-old man who had been found guilty of raping a 27-year-old woman in Chicago's Lincoln Park. The woman was paralyzed and in a wheelchair. Her companion, also in a wheelchair, fought off a second assailant and escaped.

Crosscurrents

The problems disabled people face in architectural, attitudinal, educational, legal, occupational, and personal barriers are inextricably intertwined. Attitudinal barriers are perhaps the most basic, cutting across into the others. So, too, do occupational barriers reflect the inferior preparation for work resulting from educational barriers and the architectural impediments in transportation and places of employment that prevent disabled people from getting to and entering buildings. And personal barriers may so monopolize a disabled person's time and energy that efforts to overcome other barriers are minimized.

But there are other crosscurrents. People with disabilities differ among and between themselves. They have different degrees of different kinds and combinations of disabilities. Yet, despite this diversity, they share many of the same problems and concerns. The words that deaf persons cannot hear are often difficult for people who are hard-of-hearing to understand. Legally blind individuals may be able to read large print that totally blind persons cannot, but much of importance is not available in large print and the strain of extended concentration limits the amount of reading possible. Persons with upper-arm control can wheel their own chairs while others must use motorized chairs; still, the architectural barriers remain.

Perhaps most important, the same kinds of barriers are present in some degree and to some extent regardless of the kind or severity of disability. Attitudes of nondisabled people may be just as negative for hard-of-hearing as for deaf people, for epileptic individuals as for blind persons. The education available to disabled persons may be equally inadequate regardless of the type of disability. Similarly, employment opportunities may be scarce. Housing problems confront disabled people in different ways but they are no less vexing for their diversity. A deaf person must wire his or her apartment or home for light signals to indicate doorbell and telephone rings just as a paraplegic individual must make architectural modifications in a home or locate a rare accessible apartment.

And America itself presents dazzlingly diverse cross-currents. In Berkeley, for example the radical movement of the sixties and the presence of a young and unusually liberal population has provided a climate of opportunity for disabled people. The Center for Independent Living, a leader in advocacy for disabled people, is there. The City Council recently spent $250,000 to install an elevator in City Hall so that citizens in wheelchairs could attend City Council meetings—which hundreds do. Washington, D.C., site of Gallaudet College, is likewise an unusually accessible place for deaf people. Many service agencies, including the subway and bus terminals, the train station, Alcoholics Anonymous, several churches, six libraries, the fire and police station headquarters, and even a dry cleaning establishment have teletypewriters (TTYs) so deaf people can call them. Interpreters who translate speech into sign language and vice versa are readily available, as are adult and continuing education classes. By contrast, San Francisco with its many hills is often nightmarish for persons in wheelchairs and services for deaf people are almost nonexistent in many rural areas. In a society as geographically mobile as ours, with a large proportion of the population moving to different cities and states each year, disabled people confront these diversities painfully often.

2

Abilities and Disabilities

Perhaps the most frustrating aspect of disability is how innocently it may begin. So little—a single gene, a solitary nerve, a pair of neurons, a tiny cluster of cells, a childhood illness, a momentary lapse on the road, an off-tackle lunge, a few drops of medicine—and an entire life is forever altered. Suddenly, almost everything must be rearranged—a marriage, a job, a friendship, a home, an everyday routine. So little, and so much.

The onset of a disability, particularly if it is a severe and sudden one, often produces enormous upheaval. Months, even years, are required before the change is complete, before the individual accepts the new circumstance and asks, What now? Yet, in another sense, it is never complete, for there will always linger the question, What if? and its companion, Perhaps someday? The world outside takes on new dimensions, evoking new questions, and posing new problems. The individual soon realizes that his difficulties stem as much from the environment as from the disability itself.

The almost 36 million disabled Americans vary among themselves so greatly that generalizations are exceedingly difficult to make. But we can say this: there is no such thing as a typical disabled person. There can be no psychology of disability as such because disabilities produce no firm and definable effects in any predictable way. Disabled people are no different from the rest of us except that they have disabilities, just as some of us are redheaded, tall, or shy; or perhaps I should say that disabled people are as different as the rest of us.

Are some people more susceptible to disability than others? Undoubtedly, the answer is yes. Some people expose themselves to possible injury more frequently than do others by, for example, sky-diving, skiing, racing, and participating in contact sports. But most people do not become disabled even when disaster strikes—they do recover from accidents and illness. Exposure alone cannot explain variations between people in susceptibility to disability. A second factor concerns individual variations. People perceive stressful events differently: some appraise them as challenging while others see them as threatening. The person's intelligence, verbal ability, biological and psychological thresholds of tolerance, morale, personality pattern, past experience, and feeling of control over his or her life all play a role in determining the response made to injury or illness, a response which may help determine whether a temporary condition is resolved successfully or persists to become a chronic impairment, e.g., a disability. A third factor is the extent of support available to the individual during a period of stress. The social position a person occupies may affect his perception of stress and, in theory at least, his vulnerability. Social isolation and marginality (minority-group membership, for example) may have negative effects, while close family ties, strong friendships, and ready accessibility to medical and social services may be positive influences.

This may help explain why disabilities are so much more common in deteriorating urban areas than in more stable suburban communities. For the correlations between disability rates and poverty are disturbing and dramatic: well over 50 percent of all disabled children come from families living at or below the poverty level, and this proportion is increasing.

But there is more. The same factors that contribute to disability also affect how an individual may respond to it. Strong social ties will encourage a positive, adaptive response, while isolation may result in despair and despondency following onset of a disability. Intelligent, well-educated persons may adjust quickly, while those with less confidence and preparation may require much longer to adapt. And severity of the disability greatly affects the individual's ability to obtain needed services and to overcome the effects of the impairment.

Our understanding of the phenomena surrounding disability is far from scientifically elegant: we cannot predict who will become disabled and how these people will respond to the condition. What we can do is to specify probable factors in the event, the individual, and the environment. This knowledge is potent, though limited, and if applied in a comprehensive fashion would, I believe, produce dramatic results. What it tells us is that disabilities exist not in a vacuum but in a complex web of medical, political, psychological, sociological, economic, and cultural forces. Thus, while we cannot predict with any satisfactory degree of certainty, we can describe the

likely physiological, personal, and environmental correlates of different disabilities quite well. Through this descriptive process, patterns and commonalities emerge
which paint a vivid portrait of what it means to be disabled in America today.

The danger with description, as with correlation, is that
we cannot specify causal relationships. To say that two
events are highly correlated is not to say that one causes
another. Both may be caused by a third factor unknown
to us or the two may have a complex interaction with
each other. An example is illustrative. In Sweden it is said
that there is an unusually large number of storks present
at the same time of year that the birth rate is highest. The
explanation here is obvious—babies conceived in cold
months are born in autumn—but those for the phenomena we are concerned with are more elusive. To say, for
example, that deafness causes people to be suspicious is
to assume more than is warranted. The real cause is more
likely the nervous behavior of people who do not know
how to communicate with a deaf person. Then, too, the
effect may not be suspiciousness at all but a normal reaction to an abnormal situation: a cautiousness in interpreting other people's behavior born of long experience with
missed words and misinterpreted cues. With that caveat,
let us look at disabilities and their correlates.

Hearing

The smallest bones of the body are the three ossicles in
the middle ear—the malleus, the incus, and the stapes.
They are set in motion by minute vibrations (100 times
smaller in breadth than the diameter of a hydrogen

atom) on the eardrum in response to pressure from sound waves. The ossicles, in turn, impinge upon the oval window to the cochlea, where mechanical energy is translated into neural energy. Infinitesimally small nerve fibers in the cochlea transmit this energy through the acoustic nerve to the auditory cortex in the brain.

Hearing impairment may occur along any point of this continuum. The milder losses emanate from pathologies involving the external and middle ear. A punctured eardrum, for example, or a break in the ossicular chain, might produce a loss of hearing. Otosclerosis, which affects about one in every 100 Americans, involves bony growths inhibiting the movement of the stapes. Otitis media, a common childhood problem, occurs when the middle ear becomes filled with fluid.

Pathologies of the cochlea and of the acoustic nerve (meningitis, for example) usually result in more serious impairments. The mechanical energy from the ossicles becomes blurred or stopped altogether, producing an inability to interpret sounds or to perceive them at all in the brain. The hair cells in the cochlea may fire indiscriminately, causing a ringing, or tinnitus, that "sounds" like a piercing whistle, a steady hum, or a fire alarm.

The process of aging is probably the single most common correlate of hearing loss, affecting the sensitivity of hair cells, the potency of the auditory signal sent to the brain, and the sensitivity of the auditory cortex cells themselves. But is it aging itself, or the accumulation of exposure to sound that is at cause? Some evidence suggests that the loudness of contemporary American life—the traffic, rock music, construction noise—more than the mere fact of aging is largely responsible. At the

height of the rock music movement in the early 1970s a
University of Tennessee study revealed that an extraordinarily high proportion of incoming freshmen had hearing impairments. And we do know that continual exposure to loud noise, such as that a factory worker might
experience, gradually leads to impairment of hearing.

Hearing loss ranges from mild, almost unnoticeable impairments to the total inability to hear and understand
speech and other sounds. A moderate loss is irritating,
particularly in groups where parts of conversations are
missed. A more severe loss requires the use of a hearing
aid and close concentration upon what people say. Deafness, however, changes an entire life.

Deafness is more than the inability to hear. A child
born deaf never learns language in a natural way but
must be taught, slowly and laboriously, that he has a
name, that things have names, that words combine (in
peculiar ways) to form sentences. Speech, too, must be
taught, a frustrating and extended effort to control the
muscles and blend the sounds into precise patterns. Because speech and language are long delayed, and seldom
become truly mastered and natural, the serious business
of academic learning starts too late and finishes too soon.
A child born deaf becomes an adult, still deaf, who will
always have difficulty speaking intelligibly, reading, and
stringing words together grammatically.

By contrast, deafness occurring later in life has dramatically different effects. The hearing loss may be identical
in severity but speech, language, and learning have already been established. Soldiers deafened in war often
felt their world had become dead, with all the vibrancy
and urgency everyday sounds convey lost. Simple activi-

ties of the day—chatting over coffee, talking on the telephone, watching TV and movies—suddenly become huge
obstacles. Deafened adults often face severe adjustment
problems, changes in occupation, and reevaluation of
their perceptions of themselves.

A deaf person must see what he cannot hear. Moving
lips form unheard words, telephones must be adapted to
transfer sound into sight, auditory buzzers must be
changed into or supplemented by lights, emotions must
be read on the face and in gestures rather than in the
voice. It is often like living in a glass box. A deaf person
can see through, but somehow he often cannot reach out.
People walk by, interacting with each other, and the effect is like watching a movie with the sound turned off:
the deaf person cannot understand their words nor can
he engage them easily in casual conversation. Their im-
mediacy reinforces his isolation. He feels so close yet so
far away.

A Day in the Life: Deafness

You awaken, not to sound, but to light or to the vibrations of an alarm attached to your clock. Your first
thoughts concern the weather but you cannot use the
radio to learn what you want to know; television is chancy
because you might mislipread or the newscaster may
never flash the information you need. Nor can you call a
telephone weather number to find out. Instead, you look
at the sky and hope your guess is right. While making
your morning coffee you watch the pot closely for the
steam that tells you the water is boiling. As you watch,
your ears begin to buzz in sympathy with the sounds you

know are there. The buzz will continue most of the day. You've learned to ignore it.

On your way to work you stop in at a drugstore for some cough drops. You select what you want, not asking for assistance, and deposit a dollar bill before the cashier. He says something—what you can only guess—and you nod toward the dollar, hoping that you are doing the right thing (and that he is not asking how you feel this morning). Back in your car, you watch traffic carefully, gazing often at the sideview mirror you are required by law to have, looking for a fire engine, a police car, or an ambulance you cannot hear.

At work, you smile quickly at your colleagues and begin your tasks. Conversation is never relaxed and you avoid it when you can. Although you can, with difficulty, make your voice understood, you avoid speaking whenever possible because you've learned from experience that it's smoother that way. The phone is a necessary evil and you have come to resign yourself to the lack of privacy and inevitable confusion generated by having someone else make calls for you. You lunch alone or with a trusted friend whose patience never seems to wear thin. You're resigned, too, to hurried excuses when you invite your co-workers to an after-hours party or for a drink, knowing that they would be as uncomfortable as you.

Later, you join some friends, also deaf, relaxing at last. You share with them some bitter jokes about "the hearing world," and exchange animated news about other deaf people. Later, you return home filled with the glow of friendship. There, you call a few more friends on your TTY, which enables you to type out conversations with others who have TTYs, and pick up the evening paper.

You turn first to the sports page, later to the news section, and ignore most of the rest. Words jump out at you but your eyes are too tired to look them up in the dictionary and you know that even if you did the definitions and synonyms would be as elusive as the words themselves.

All of this time, your wife and children come in and out of the room, signing questions and requests, she naturally and they with effort because they can hear and she cannot. You want the best for them, and feel frustrated once again that your deafness interferes with getting higher-paying jobs that require constant conversations in person and on the phone. You wish you could take your wife to a movie or a play, but know it would be pointless. Feeling guilty, you find her, give her a kiss, and lead her to bed. Her warmth is comforting and soon you're lost in sleep.

Seeing

The eye, like the ear, translates energy. Light waves impinging upon the cornea are changed to neural energy which traverses the optic nerves to the occipital cortex in the brain. The number of neurons specialized for vision greatly exceeds that for any other sense. In fact, almost one-fourth of the brain's energy is expended on vision.

Visual impairments may be caused by infections, tumors, injuries and accidents, glaucoma, cataracts, poisoning, and prenatal conditions (including heredity). Like hearing, vision generally declines with age. Structural anomalies (myopia, albinism, etc.) of the eyeball, dislocated lenses, retinal problems, optic nerve degeneration, and occipital cortex damage may all be involved.

Refractive errors comprise about half of all visual impairments. These involve cases in which the image does not focus on the retina normally, producing nearsightedness or farsightedness, astigmatism (a blurring of vision resulting from light rays focusing on different parts of the retina), crossed eyes, and muscular imbalances causing the eyes to deviate from their normal positions. Cataracts are a clouding of the lens in which visual acuity is reduced as the lens becomes increasingly opaque. Other diseases and conditions can attack the eye, the nerves, or the occipital cortex and produce loss of visual acuity. Retrolental fibroplasia (RLF), caused by excessive oxygen administered to premature newborns placed in incubators, left in its wake thousands of blinded infants before its cause was found in 1954.

Impairments of vision range from mild losses to total blindness in which even light perception is absent. Persons whose vision is impaired may require corrective lenses, which often produce normal vision. While a hearing aid distorts sound (for which reason many hearing-impaired persons reject it), glasses or contact lenses properly fitted rarely distort light perception. Lack of correction or improperly fitted lenses, however, may result in headaches, nausea, and early exhaustion of the eyes. Most visual impairments are correctable through surgery or prescription lenses and the individual is usually able to resume a normal life, although relationships with others may be altered somewhat and self-image negatively affected. Blindness, however, produces dramatic and enduring changes in a person's entire life.

Blindness occurring at birth or early in childhood affects a child's ability to form accurate perceptions of himself and of the world around him. Emotions must be read in the voice, and because people are usually more adept at masking their true emotions in speech than in gestures and posture, this might lead a child or an adult to misinterpret feelings and intentions. There is, however, no conclusive evidence that blind individuals differ from sighted persons in language use, personality, intelligence, auditory acuity, musical ability, or academic achievement. Myths persist, but these lack validity.

The disability does, however, have definite effects upon an individual's activities, interactions with others, and self-perception. It restricts activity by limiting access to the printed word, mobility in unfamiliar places, perception of the environment, and understanding of social cues. Interaction with others is hampered largely by their attitudes and emotions, rather than by the blind person's own. Not being able to see others and through this process to measure himself against them, the blind person's self-image may develop almost solely in relation to what he or she hears others say and do.

The "obstacle sense" that so often bewilders sighted individuals has a simple explanation. Blind people cannot hear better than others can, but they have generally learned to make greater use of what they hear. Sound waves instigated by a cane or other object (most often, a shoe) hitting the pavement bounce off nearby objects and return, rising in pitch as objects come closer, enabling the blind individual to judge his distance from them. Only about 5 percent of the blind population uses guide dogs, about the same proportion that reads Braille, both percentages seeming unexpectedly low to a public accustomed to thinking that most blind people do both. But guide dogs don't guide, just warn of nearby obstacles that an experienced traveler can perceive through sound wave variations, and Braille is slow and usually unnecessary because most legally blind people can read large print and those who can't may obtain most information they need in conversation or on recordings.

A Day in the Life: Blindness

At the sudden sound of the clock radio, you open your eyes immediately and automatically. The announcer is describing the weather—cloudy with a 40 percent chance of rain—and the first thought to hit your mind is not "cool" but "dark," because you've been taught that way, just as you've been taught to keep your eyes open even though you see little if anything with them, to think in terms of light and vision as well as the other sensory perceptions you yourself experience, to face others when they talk to you rather than turning an ear to the sound of their voice. None of these things came naturally but your teachers explained that these concessions to sighted persons would enhance their acceptance of you. For similar reasons, you automatically use phrases like "I see" and "It looks like. . . ."

You select your clothes quickly, knowing exactly where each item is (browns together, etc.) and feeling the fabric just to be sure. Another trick is to label each item with a small Brailled description, but you've found this is not necessary, and the bother of putting on and removing the labels each time is just that—a bother. It's so simple, you think, wondering again why people so often ask you how you do it. Color coordination of suit, shirt, tie, socks, and shoes is as much a matter of rote as of taste: you've memorized acceptable combinations, though sometimes you enjoy experimenting rebelliously.

Problems do not begin until you're on unfamiliar ground. In the apartment, in the building, and around the block you know exactly where everything is. Flipping the glass case of your watch, you feel the time, and quicken your pace a bit so you will not miss the 8:25 bus to the office. Arriving at the corner, you hear a neighbor telling you your bus hasn't arrived. Someone always volunteers information, they're rather conscientious about it. Children sometimes try to mislead you as a joke, but their voices give away the lie.

At work by 9:00, the receptionist calls "Hi" a bit too loudly. Most people do, until you tell them nothing's wrong with your ears, and even then they slip occasionally, especially if they are nervous or you are facing the other way. At 9:30 a woman appears for an appointment. From her voice, you guess she's relatively young (the tone is clear and the pitch moderately high) and about 5 feet 4 inches tall (the sound comes from below your ears). You turn to face her, by habit again, and smile a welcome. And then you wait for more cues—is she in a rush, nervous, businesslike, or chatty? She tells you she went to school with a blind boy once and then you begin your discussion. You smile as she stops after saying, "Have you read ...," accustomed to the self-consciousness of sighted people talking about things they can see. In the company cafeteria for lunch, she insists on describing what is available, all of it, though what you need to know is what's different today and at what price. Still, you're glad most people make the effort. It's mostly reaction rather than action: if you asked them to join you after work, there would be an excuse.

So far, the day has been routine. But now you must venture to a new location for an afternoon meeting. You call for a cab, listen for rain, and wait at the curb. A bus would be cheaper but much too time-consuming. Arriving, you walk slowly and unsurely, your cane swinging rapidly, trying to find out what's where. And you readily accept guiding arms you would decline at home or in the office. It's a long meeting, a lot of new voices, tiring. When it's over, you realize it's too late to go back to the office so you can catch your bus home, so you take a cab all the way home.

Your wife has dinner ready when you arrive. After dinner, she reads the paper aloud and you add details you've heard at the office. A few TV shows, with her supplying helpful commentary, a radio program, with you alerting her to sounds she didn't know she heard. Later, in bed, you wonder if you'd have been more successful if you could have seen, more aggressive perhaps, more relaxed, less dependent. All in all, you're doing okay. The day was a good one and tomorrow will be too.

Moving

Our nervous systems extend from the brain down the spinal cord and out through peripheral nerves to the extremities of the body. The motor cortex, just in front of the fissure of Rolando in the frontal lobe, regulates voluntary movements. In the right hemisphere, this cortex controls the left side of the body; in the left, the right side. The two hemispheres are connected in the corpus callosum. Cortical cells representing the muscles of different parts of the body are proportional in magnitude not to the muscle groups or to body size but to the degree of fine motor control achieved. Thus, the fingers and lips are heavily represented, while the trunk is comparatively slighted.

Information from the brain is received, processed, and transmitted by the spinal cord to the periphery for the initiation and control of motor activity. Efferent neurons transmit energy to muscles, while afferent neurons carry messages from them. Interneurons intervene between these specialized neurons, greatly increasing the complexity of possible muscle action.

Neurological conditions, most prominently cerebral palsy, epilepsy, and spina bifida, and orthopedic disabilities, primarily those associated with polio, arthritis, muscular dystrophy, and spinal cord injuries may restrict an individual's mobility. In paraplegia, the legs are affected; in quadriplegia, all four limbs are; and in hemiplegia, one side of the body is involved.

Cerebral palsy—the name means "a motor disability in the brain"—may influence not only gross and fine motor control but also perception, learning, language, and speech. Typically, some degree of paralysis, weakness, and lack of coordination results. Most cerebral palsied individuals are spastic rather than athetoid—that is, the muscles are involuntarily tensed rather than writhing, although both conditions may produce jerky and uncontrolled movements. Because the same etiologies lead to cerebral palsy and mental retardation, the two disabilities are often present in the same person, but one does not cause the other: cerebral palsied people may be intellectually gifted and retarded people need not be palsied. Still, because of shared etiologies between cerebral palsy and many other disabilities, cerebral palsied individuals typically are multiply disabled.

Epilepsy—"to be seized"—results when a group of brain cells is disturbed by an injury that causes them to discharge their electrical energy convulsively or from a genetic condition. High fevers, head injuries, infections, and oxygen or blood disruptions may produce epilepsy and there is some evidence the disability may be inherited. The convulsions, or seizures, may be grand mal or petit mal, although two other, much rarer, types have been identified. In a grand mal seizure the individual may experience a warning "aura" (he may smell, hear, see, or feel unusual sensations) after which a stiffness and a subsequent series of contractions occur. Following the attack the person falls asleep. In a petit mal seizure the individual may not even know he is having an attack so fleeting is the seizure. Since the advent of modern drugs, particularly Dilatin, most grand mal and petit mal seizures can be controlled.

Spina bifida, as the name implies, is a spinal condition in which the spine never completely closes. A congenital defect, it may produce paralysis of the legs and an inability to control the bowel and sphincter. Affected individuals can usually learn to walk with braces or crutches, or move about in a wheelchair, although incontinence persists.

Poliomyelitis, now rare due to the development of vaccines, occurs when a virus attacks the gray matter of the spine, resulting in paralysis. Arthritis, which usually occurs in middle or old age, involves inflammation of the joints caused by infection or metabolism changes. Muscular dystrophy is a progressive disease in which muscle fibers are gradually replaced by fatty tissue causing a weakening of muscles and usually death by adolescence or early adulthood. Spinal cord injuries may occur in automobile accidents, in sporting events, or in other violent collisions, and usually result in paralysis of some part or parts of the body.

It is difficult to generalize about such a diverse set of disabilities. But it is probably safe to conclude, as have many neurologically and orthopedically impaired individuals, that their primary problems are social rather than physical. This is especially true of persons with epilepsy, who have been feared, scorned, and discriminated against for centuries. Social rejection may in turn lead to lowered self-concepts, which then affect the individuals' motivation to succeed. The primary problem other than social acceptance is mobility. It is here that architectural and transportation barriers make their most devastating impact.

A Day in the Life: Paraplegia

You slip off the bed into the waiting chair and wheel to the bathroom where you dismount onto a specially designed toilet seat. Remounting, you begin combing your hair and making up, using the floor-length mirror on the bathroom door. Your toilet articles and makeup are all on the platform or on low-level shelves. Returning to the bedroom, you select your clothes and begin to dress. This entire process has taken half an hour. At last, you enter the kitchen, removing instant coffee from a low cabinet and straining to fill the pot with water. In each room you must jump to reach the light switch to turn it on and off. Two or three times this hour you raise your body by pushing on the armrests so you can change position slightly and momentarily relieve the pressure on your hipbones.

At the front door you release the lock, grasp the handle, and with your free hand wheel the chair backwards. Holding the door open with one hand, you wheel through with the other, turn and lock the door. A long hallway, an elevator, and another door. The pavement is just three steps down but you must wheel the length of the building, ease down a slope, and return.

You open the car door as you do most other doors, and slip onto the front seat. You collapse the chair and fit it between the front and rear seats. You start the car using hand controls and begin your trip to work. There, you reverse the process, arriving at last at your desk. As long as you stay there, you have no special limitations. Today is a good day with no particular problems other than the usual struggle with the bathroom doors (two doors, one barely four feet behind the other; once you were trapped there, unable to turn around). And, as happens almost every day, a visitor to the office passes by and whistles, only to blush with embarrassment when he sees the chair. It's been like that ever since, as a high school cheerleader en route to a football game, a car came out of nowhere and struck you down. The hardest part is always to forget the appreciative first smiles because they never really return, and to stop the idle dreams of what might have been.

You lunch at your desk—it's infinitely easier—and the afternoon drags on. You think about women's liberation, trying not to hear the conversations around you, and wonder when you will ever be treated fully as a woman. That is what hurts, even more than the exhaustion of moving about. People think, falsely, and without asking, that you must be incapable of having sex, and sometimes just assume you have no feelings for it at all. Shopping is always a hassle, especially with anti-theft bars at supermarkets, so you decide to put that off until the weekend when there will be time enough to visit more than one or two stores. It's been two weeks now and tomorrow you must get supplies for another week or two.

Tonight, however, you have an important meeting to attend—the mayor has promised to be there and your group will present him with demands for architectural and transportation barrier removal. It takes you an hour and a half to get to the meeting, but the mayor cancels his appearance. So you end up talking to each other once again. Another hour to get home and you're exhausted. Tomorrow? Oh, the shopping. You hope you'll be too tired to go.

Learning and Thinking

Aristotle's leap, two thousand years in the making, is still not complete. We do not yet know how we learn or how we think, or why some people learn or think better than others do. Learning occurs, it seems, when a chemical or neurophysiological change alters certain cells and the ways they interact with each other. Some exciting work suggests that these changes may occur in RNA (riboneucleic acid). RNA is a large molecule found in almost all cells that apparently stores new information much the way DNA (deoxyriboneucleic acid) stores hereditary information. Lamarck, of course, was wrong about the inheritance of acquired traits, but is the RNA-DNA dichotomy one reason? Many scientists insist on a neurophysiological theory of learning in which some rearrangement of neural interactions is responsible for learning. Certainly it is not a matter of the sheer number of cells or nerves (the largest brain ever recorded belonged to a profoundly retarded individual) but it may involve the complexity of neural (or synaptic) networks in the cerebrum. How we think is even less apparent: we do know that to think we must have information, but until we know how that information is processed, stored, and retrieved, it is unlikely we will understand much about how learning is related to thinking.

Recent research has focused upon the role of what are called "neurotransmitters," which are substances believed to transmit messages from one nerve cell to another. Three such chemicals found in the brain—dopamine, serotonin, and norepinephrine—have been identified and others are being sought. While scientists previously believed that nerve messages were transmitted from cell to cell by impulses that traversed the synapses between cells, it now appears that the message travels only to the end of one cell, at which point a neurotransmitter is released that crosses the synapse and stimulates the adjacent nerve. Although much remains to be learned, it now seems that neurotransmitters are involved in learning, memory, movement, and even in mental illness.

Causes of mental retardation and of specific learning disabilities are similarly shrouded in mystery. The best we can do, it seems, is to identify probable etiologies for about 10 percent of the cases. Heredity is undoubtedly one cause, as is birth injury, and many of the same diseases that result in sensory deprivation may also attack the brain itself. Glandular imbalances are known to be involved. It is also recognized that older mothers are more likely to give birth to mentally impaired children than are younger mothers. Environmental causes, including malnutrition, are undeniably important.

Mental disabilities may affect only one area of functioning (writing, for example) or may result in generalized difficulties. Specific learning disabilities appear to result from deficiencies in specialized parts of the brain— Broca's area for speech, the prefrontal lobe for creativity, for example. In general learning disabilities, on the other hand, the deficiency is diffused, permeating the functioning of the brain as a whole. While general learning disabilities are more or less readily detected by means of intelligence tests, determination of the presence in an individual of a specific learning disability has proven much more elusive. The definitions now in use are so nebulous that Congress, in enacting the Education for All Handicapped Children Act of 1975, intentionally took the unusual step of placing an upper limit on the number of children who could be labeled learning disabled (who could be said to have specific learning disabilities).

To speculate for a moment, it may be that learning and thinking involve both chemical and neurophysiological actions. An experience transmitted by the senses to the brain may somehow result in a cluster of cells forging into a unit. We do know that as one cell repeatedly excites another the amount of energy needed to cause one of them to fire (nerve cells fire on an all-or-none basis) is reduced. Mental disabilities may be related, under this theory, to excitation potentials (the amount of energy required for firing), synaptic junctures between nerve cells, and chemical composition of the cells themselves, perhaps including RNA, as these are affected by genetic, glandular, disease, injury, and other conditions. But we are not likely to know what causes mental disabilities, and how they come about, for years to come.

Mental disabilities may be mild, moderate, severe, and profound. Mildly retarded individuals may learn basic academic skills up to approximately the sixth-grade level; moderately retarded persons to the second-grade level; severely impaired individuals may learn minimal self-help skills; and profoundly retarded persons may require life-long institutional care. People who have specific learning disabilities, such as those affecting reading or writing, are usually limited only in the impaired capacity; they can often learn to compensate through other, unimpaired, means. Much depends upon how soon intervention is initiated and how the individual is helped. The great majority of mentally disabled persons can contribute to their own care and support and can live lives that have meaning for themselves and for others. Specific learning disabilities are not usually connected to general learning disabilities. Albert Einstein, for example, had a specific learning disability, as did Winston Churchill and many other famous people. Yet they had superior intelligence.

A Day in the Life: Mild Retardation

You awaken with a smile, remembering fleetingly your dream: you were a halfback idolized by the whole community. You've always loved sports and physical activity and today you're excited about a new kind of physical exertion. Your father, an old man now, has promised to introduce you to a friend who works in a steel plant. You want to show your father and his friend how well you can work—maybe you'll get a job at last.

The basic chores are habit by now: you do them as well as anyone, concentrating on them more intensely perhaps, but getting them done. You shower, dress, clean your room (it's spotless), and straighten out the rest of the house. Soon it's time to go. Your father drives you, reminding you along the way not to seem too eager, to control yourself. The Saturday morning sunlight warms you and you feel confident about your chances. At the plant, your father talks with his friend but you are too excited to listen. Besides, many of their words make no sense.

Soon, you're watching a job being done. The assembly line brings cold steel bars one by one, dumping them in a curved receptacle. Your father's friend quickly ties the bars together on both ends, wraps a red identifying tag on the bundle, and releases the receptacle so the bars roll to one side, where another worker readies them for the crane to hoist onto a waiting truck. The job is simple enough, you think—the man said something about it being very boring for some people—and you watch him do it again and again. Then you're ready to try. It takes a few dozen mistakes before you've got the routine down pat, but there's no doubt in your mind that you could do the job.

You and your father leave happily and drive into town to do some shopping. You've done this many times before, and you know he appreciates your help. On the road again, he tells you that he believes you will be able to live independently of him should you get this or some other job. You're not sure you would like that, but you nod. It's true: most things you can do, even if sometimes you need help. Social relations are more difficult, but you know you can learn that too in time.

The afternoon passes quickly. You mow the lawn, make some repairs, and watch some football games on TV. You make dinner for the two of you and it's good. Later you ask your father many questions about the steel plant, hungry to learn all you can. At last it's time for bed—and more dreams. But this time they're about working.

Feeling

In the battle between reason and emotion, emotion usually wins. Conflict, anxiety, fear, frustration, anger, pain, fatigue, love, hatred, joy, and sadness are potent feelings that may surface quickly and disappear as suddenly or may remain over long periods of time. We may suppress them or manufacture camouflages but we cannot long escape them. In time, their suppression may produce psychosomatic diseases and symptoms such as ulcers, high blood pressure, kidney disease, and "hysteria"—the sudden inability to do something. A singer under great stress may be unable to speak, a child anxious about school might be unable to hear, an athlete apprehensive about defeat might be unable to walk. A patient with hysteria is not malingering; he really believes he cannot perform.

All of us live with stress. For constitutional or environmental reasons, some of us may be or have learned to be less susceptible to it than are others. All of us employ rationalization and other defense mechanisms to protect ourselves from having to face unpleasant facts. But some of us suffer from more intense or chronic stress than do others. In children, emotional disturbance may result from uncertainty or instability in the family or from conflicting messages from parents. The child may exhibit bizarre behavior or may withdraw from human interaction, as in autism, perhaps inflicting pain and injury upon himself. Mental illness results in retreat from reality. In schizophrenia, extreme apathy and sometimes delusions are evident.

Some behavioral disorders have identifiable genetic, constitutional, or organic etiologies. Toxic substances affecting the brain may be the cause. Neurological imbalances may be involved, particularly in the limbic system of the forebrain. But we are much more confident, it seems, in identifying environmental causes, including stress and parental attention to deviant behavior. Drugs are known to produce emotional disabilities, particularly if taken over a considerable period of time.

Emotionally disabled individuals may be helped with certain drugs, through therapy, and by environmental engineering (also known as behavior modification). Persons who have regained an acceptable level of control after being seriously impaired are referred to as "mentally restored." They are no longer dangers to themselves or to society in normal life circumstances. Other individuals may regain considerable control but may need continuing assistance periodically for some time until they are able to function normally. Our society often appears less interested in helping emotionally disabled persons than in hiding them in hospitals. Emotional impairments are particularly frightening to many people because they do not understand what is happening or might happen.

A Day in the Life: Incipient Mental Illness

You awaken, as usual these past few weeks, to a headache. And for the fourth time this week, you're going to be late to work. You dress in a hurry, gulping down some coffee as you apply eye shadow. Then, just as you are dressed, a sudden move for a forgotten scarf and the coffee cup drops, staining the yellow plaid dress. Staring at yourself in the mirror, you are suddenly helpless, feeling rage and dejection at once. What is happening to me? you ask yourself, not once but repeatedly.

The shock of the baby's death at two months, a "crib death" the doctor said, but no one ever learned why, the horror of it and the aching void it left, the pain of remembering something each time you pass the baby's room, the self-incrimination that never ends. You could not really blame Bob for leaving you, convinced of your negligence or worse, because there was really no justification that could be offered for what had happened.

An hour later, still tense, you begin the day at the sewing plant. A cut finger is all it takes. Your tears are stopped by four other women, and you ask to rest. Back on the job, the same motions again and again, cutting material, guiding it through the machine, you lose track of time.

Your superior calls you into his office. You try to explain—I was just nervous, I'll not do it again—but you can see he is disturbed. This time, you get off with a warning, but next time? You don't need this pressure, not with your problems. Think about what you're doing. Six across, three down, there, you've got it.

The apartment is forbiddingly lonely that night. You find your dress on the floor, the broken cup nearby. They'll keep. You take some sleeping pills to forget and end another day.

Talking

Air streams up from the lungs into the larynx where the vocal folds open and close rapidly to produce sound which is then refined in the pharyngeal, oral, and nasal cavities. That is speech. But it is much more than just this: anatomical, sociological, psychological, and educational factors all contribute to speech. In the brain, the frontal lobe, particularly Broca's area, is concerned with speech production, and Wernicke's area in the parieto-temporal lobe juncture with auditory monitoring of speech. Social pressure, inadequate speech models, and faulty speech training may negatively affect speech quality, just as may poor self-concept and nervousness. The multitude of factors leads us to suspect that speech disorders are common: they are.

Organic causes of speech disabilities include cleft palate, mouth or jaw irregularities, missing or malformed teeth, muscular paralysis in the larynx, tumors, brain damage, and nasal obstructions. Functional etiologies include personality, emotional, and educational deficiencies. Many speech-disabled individuals have other disorders, such as retardation and cerebral palsy. And hearing impairment interferes with speech development by limiting comprehension of the speech of others and of the individual himself: unable to model his speech or to monitor it, the deaf person must be taught speech slowly and laboriously.

Speech disorders relate to disturbances in articulation, voice production, rhythm (stuttering, stammering, cluttering), neurology (chiefly hearing and mental retardation associated disorders), and cleft palate. Speech may be absent altogether, echolalic (mindless repetition), slurred, halting, hoarse, harsh, almost inaudible, or excessively loud.

The effects of speech disabilities are largely social and personal. Others may find the speech unpleasant and may avoid the disabled individual, who may in turn lower his or her self-concept. Difficulties in speaking may lead a person to withdraw from social interaction and may negatively affect his or her motivation to learn and to work with others. Speech therapy, while frustrating, extended, and often boring, can be fruitful.

A Day in the Life: Stuttering

You arise and prepare for work uneventfully. In the car you go over what you plan to say at the meeting this morning, practicing to yourself and building your confidence. It's always like this, which is why you're sometimes slow in responding to others: you've found that if you frame your answer beforehand, you're less likely to stutter. This morning you're nervous about the meeting and you do stutter, but only once or twice. Afterward, you're quite pleased with yourself.

So much can trigger stuttering—confusion about the question, uncertainty about the answer, nervousness, pressure, and excitement. In the typical day you face all of these. Your therapist taught you to slow down, and for months you said everything with a deliberation that seemed ridiculous, but it worked. What used to be habitual is only occasional now and the next step is to make it extinct.

That's important because the job you want is a managerial position that involves constant talking and a good deal of tension. You've been locked in your job for five years and the time has come to move up. You know the boss worries about bad impressions on customers, so you resolve to redouble your efforts. By Christmas, you promise yourself, you'll have it by then.

It surprises you constantly how touchy people are about speech. Even a slight difference from the sounds they are accustomed to hear, and they are disturbed. It's especially hard for you to get dates because your would-be boyfriends are nervous about the stuttering. One answer would be to talk as little as possible, but that would be negative. You're tired of stuttering and of the way it has changed your life.

At the hardware store after work, the cashier looks at you strangely when you ask how much the thumbtacks are. You're angry that you cannot command a cashier's respect, and all the way home you lecture yourself on speaking slowly and distinctly. Then you remember what the therapist said: take it easy, too much worry only makes it worse. And again you wonder, is there a right balance in there somewhere?

The evening is easy—no one to talk to—lonely. You watch TV, trying to forget the day and the cashier. Must every day be like this? You pick up the book *Speech Can Change Your Life,* and when you finish reading you remember the progress you made at the meeting and know the answer is no.

Multiple Disabilities

Because etiologies are common across several disabilities, a single cause may result in multiple disability. Meningitis, for example, can produce deafness and mental impairment; similarly, rubella (German measles in a pregnant woman) can produce blindness, deafness, cerebral palsy, and mental retardation in her child. And because disabled people are as likely as are nondisabled individuals to have injuries and illnesses, they may become disabled in yet other ways. The fact is that the disabled population of this country is rapidly becoming a multiply disabled group of people. Already, half of all disabled children and youth of school age are multiply disabled, with fully one-fourth having three or more disabilities. And each succeeding year, more and more school-age children are multiply disabled.

The needs of multiply disabled children, youth, and adults are not being met in America today. In fact, we have barely begun even to understand the scope of the problems these people face. The barriers confronting them are enormous even in comparison with those met by other disabled persons. While service programs and community acceptance of disabled individuals leave much to be desired, they have a world to offer compared with what is available to many multiply disabled people. As a result, many of these persons are institutionalized and even there receive tragically inadequate care.

It is when we attempt to meet the needs of these people that the fragmented and compartmentalized nature of our service delivery systems hits us with greatest force. No one, it seems, is ready to accept these people. Each program has its own definitions, its own qualifications for eligibility, its own priorities—and its own limited capacities. Multiply disabled persons are typically shuttled from one program to another, vainly, only to meet rejection each time. Even disabled people themselves often seem unwilling to advocate for others than their own, and multiply disabled people are always someone else's problem.

Compounding the difficulty is the fact that multiply disabled people are a bewilderingly diverse lot. Treatment must often be on a one-to-one basis or even on a two-, three-, or four-to-one basis, with numerous specialists combining their talents and knowledge to help a single person. There can be no doubt that educating and rehabilitating multiply disabled people is usually expensive, time-consuming, and very difficult.

But this can be no excuse. If we believe in the dignity of the individual, if we are willing to help a mildly disabled person reach his or her potential, we must be ready to go all the way, because even the most severely disabled person is as important as is anyone else. We tend to forget, when we see the awesome disabilities, that this person has potential to achieve and to contribute, a potential defined not by his or her disabilities but by abilities. And we must reach those abilities, free them, and let the individual stand as tall as he or she can. To do otherwise is to handicap the person, and by depriving us of his or her contributions, to handicap America.

Incidence, Prevalence, and Definitions

I have purposely avoided providing data on the incidence (number of new cases annually) and prevalence (number of existing instances) for the disabilities discussed in this chapter. Some of the reasons are discussed in Chapter 5, which takes up educational barriers, but a word or two is in order here.

The sobering fact is that we do not know, even within acceptable limitations, how many Americans have any one or combination of disabilities. The estimates fluctuate widely and wildly. Definitions diverge from study to study, year to year, state to state, school to school, person to person. Diagnosis is often uncertain, as witness the questions of what is a learning disability, who has one, and how do we decide that? As a result, misdiagnoses occur frighteningly often. A deaf child's lack of speech may lead a physician to a diagnosis of mental retardation—muteness in childhood is characteristic of both disabilities—and to a recommendation of institutionalization. And this has happened: we have discovered 40-year-old persons who have wrongly spent 35 or more years in state hospitals because of exactly this mistake.

We have tolerated this situation for far too long. Our physicians receive too little training in diagnosis and re-

mediation of disabilities, particularly in the area of referral for more intensive treatment. If often seems to be the
rule more than the exception for parents to have to con-
sult two or more doctors before an accurate assessment is
made, for a physician's recommendations for treatment
and assistance to be inadequate if not totally misleading,
for educators and other service workers to disagree in
their definitions of disability and in their plans for remediation. No wonder parents so often become baffled and
bewildered, children so often are poorly educated, adults
so often become welfare recipients instead of productive
workers.

The United States Office of Education estimates that
approximately one million children and youth who have
disabilities are out of school altogether—and no one
knows who they are, where they live, or what they need.
The Bureau of Labor Statistics does not even attempt to
collect and report data on employment among disabled
people. The Census will not even count these people until
1980, although it did make a small, limited effort in 1970
when it asked a 5-percent sampling questions about disability.

We cannot help people until we know who they are,
where they live, what disabilities they have, and what abilities and interests they exhibit. Our lack of knowledge
about these people reflects a lack of serious concern. Disabled people remain out of the mainstream of American
life and will not enter it until we make strenuous efforts
to admit them. Definitions and statistics are parts of the
problem of handicapping America. They are also parts of
the solution.

3

You Can't Get There from Here

A mother pushing a carriage . . . a father struggling with Christmas presents . . . a tight end hobbling on a sprained ankle . . . a pregnant woman . . . an arthritic elderly man . . . a blind attorney . . . a deaf teacher . . . a paraplegic editor . . . a young child.

A flight of stairs . . . a narrow doorway . . . a small bathroom . . . shoulder-height light switches . . . an inclined slope . . . chest-level drinking fountains . . . thoughtlessly designed playgrounds . . . waist-high kitchen appliances . . . escalators . . . high bus steps . . . underground subways . . . eye-level telephones . . . narrow theater aisles . . . auditory fire alarms . . . chest-high keyholes . . . highly polished floors . . . tight parking spaces . . . head-level mirrors . . . printed directions and maps . . . heat-sensitive elevator call buttons . . . eye-level cabinets.

Tens of millions of Americans—estimates range from a low of 14 million to a high of 50 million—have mobility limitations. And these numbers do not include children who cannot reach high cabinets or negotiate bus stairs, pregnant women, mothers wheeling carriages, and others who face more temporary restrictions.

Architects and engineers have designed an America to meet the needs of the average, able-bodied, right-handed adult, and only now are beginning to realize the colossal dimensions of their errors. Parents and community residents stood by passively and acquiesced unwittingly to the man-made barriers that daily affect their lives. Architectural and transportation barriers of our own creation handicap America.

Virtually every building and every road, every curb and every stair, every doorway and every aisle sooner or later will prevent someone from moving along his intended path.

Ramps don't cost that much more than stairs—until you have the stairs in place. Thirty-two-inch doors are not extravagant compared with narrower ones—until you must cut through masonry and steel. Indeed, a nationwide study by the National League of Cities revealed that the increase in cost between construction of inaccessible buildings and those that would be totally accessible to every American may be as little as one percent. But before the change will be made we must revolutionize entrenched practices of ponderous bureaucracies—in many ways a harder, more expensive, and qualitatively more constrained task than cutting through masonry and steel.

For the pattern is depressingly familiar. Plans are drawn for a building, funds allocated, construction begun, the edifice opened—and only then does someone "notice" that the building is inaccessible to people in wheelchairs, dangerous to deaf persons who cannot hear warning signals, and treacherous for blind persons who cannot find their way around. Disabled people mobilize to demand accessibility as their right under law, since the construction was financed with federal funds (almost all public buildings and many private ones receive at least some federal financial assistance, usually through loans). The builders then point to prohibitive cost figures for retrofitting the existing structure, and the battle is on.

Yet none of this is necessary. Involvement of representatives of all potential users of a structure from the beginning adds little to a building's total cost but greatly expands its value to the community. It may, in fact, even result in savings. Removing soil and installing stairs, for example, may be more expensive than using the soil already there to design a gently inclining slope to the front door. A transportation system designed for use by all Americans attracts more riders, increasing revenue. Accessible buildings and vehicles reduce safety hazards, producing lower insurance premiums. And most important, the right of every American to live where he chooses, move where he pleases, visit his elected representatives, vote, receive an education, and work may be assured. A more equitable, cost-beneficial approach to design is difficult to imagine. Yet the construction project that proceeds in this fashion is an isolated exception. The puzzling question is, Why?

Architectural Barriers

American architecture today is vigorous, experimental, diverse, and provocative. The names alone of creative architects evoke myriad images of exciting innovation: Frank Lloyd Wright, R. Buckminster Fuller, I. M. Pei,

Ludwig Mies van der Rohe, Louis I. Kahn. Some are rational and structural, some more sculptural in their design. Most recognize their dual responsibilities to art and to society, to themselves and to the people for whom they build.

Yet the overall quality of modern American architecture leaves much to be desired. The World Trade Center buildings in New York City are striking to look at but often overwhelmingly oppressive to their tenants. To be modern, it seems, is to be minimal and starkly functional. The suburbs are stupefying in their sameness, and urban development projects are monotonously mediocre. There is precious little planning and as a result we face accelerating chaos. We hail our efforts to build low-income housing, but the facts are tragic: we tear down more units than we build and those we build seem to deteriorate more rapidly than did those we destroy. Architecture in America has failed both art and society.

Nowhere is this failure more striking than in the area of accessibility. Ralph Rapson's use of environmental space is unforgettable, but did he ever think of the sheer diversity of people who would use his Tyrone Guthrie Theatre in Minneapolis—or of the people who cannot now use it? Did Benjamin Thompson, chairman of Harvard's Department of Architecture, consider wheelchairs when he planned his beloved stairs?

For architecture affects all aspects of the lives of all Americans—the schools they attend or cannot attend, the workplaces where they obtain a job or are denied employment, the transportation terminals they pass through or must be helped around, the recreational facilities they use or must pass by. The fact is that America's architects have designed barriers at every turn. From the Lincoln Memorial's imposing array of steps to the long passageways of the Pan American terminal at Kennedy International Airport to the narrow doorways of countless structures, many buildings have flagrantly inaccessible features. It is not for a lack of quality in architectural firms. In 1961, for example, 256 firms submitted plans for Boston's proposed City Hall. The winning entry of Kallman, McKinnell, and Knowles was praised by the city council and by fellow architects as daring yet classical, vigorous and unified, dramatic and contrasting, altogether a structure achieving great monumentality. It was also inaccessible.

Architectural accessibility involves factors essential for disabled persons to enter and use a building, factors which also facilitate entry and use by many nondisabled persons. Yet a 1967 study by the National Commission on Architectural Barriers (NCAB) found that only 3 percent of 278 cities and 4 percent of 124 counties had prepared building codes that allowed for accessibility to all persons and identified only six states that even specified what was meant by the word accessibility. If NCAB had attempted to count accessible buildings, the results might have been even more dismal.

That was six years after the publication in 1961 by the American National Standards Association (now the American National Standards Institute, or ANSI) of standards for accessibility. The standards, among other things, presented such basic design features as: (1) at least one ground-level entrance to a building; (2) the use of ramps in at least one location; (3) doorways 32 inches wide or wider; (4) restrooms which can accommodate wheelchairs; (5) access to elevators; and (6) safe parking for disabled persons. The NCAB study made it apparent that the ANSI standards were not being complied with by builders. While not comprehensive—the standards focus upon wheelchair accessibility, giving little attention to the needs of other disabled persons and to able-bodied individuals with special, temporary needs—the ANSI standards nevertheless represented a needed change that was not being made.

In 1968 the force of law was placed behind the ANSI standards by the Architectural Barriers Act of 1968 (P. L. 90–480). All federally financed public buildings were to be designed for accessibility to physically disabled persons. The law authorized the Administrator of the General Services Administration (GSA) to promulgate standards for accessibility. GSA officially adopted the ANSI standards rather than create new ones, so now the 1961 standards were enforceable.

Yet they were not enforced. Large loopholes in the loosely worded law permitted builders to escape compliance. The law applied only to federally financed efforts started after the law took effect and to renovations made after that date with federal assistance. Still, many legislators and disabled people expected more from architects and engineers—recognition of the needs of disabled people, of the essential logic in designing for all Americans, and of the small increase in costs involved. That so few complied with the law or followed its example indicated that a potent compliance effort would be needed.

Transportation Barriers

The Architectural Barriers Act made no mention of access to transportation services. In 1970 Mario Biaggi, a Congressman from New York City, succeeded in attaching an amendment to the 1964 Urban Mass Transportation Act. The amendment (P. L. 91–453) called for a national policy that elderly and disabled people have the right to the same access to transportation as do other groups in America. It required "special efforts" by designers and builders to accomplish this.

Again, there was no enforcement provision, and again, loose language (what, for example, does "special efforts" mean?) permitted contractors to ignore the law. Mass transit planners continued to design narrow doors, high steps to platforms, little room for maneuverability, and inaccessible transportation terminals. Equally important, few efforts were made to ensure that deaf, blind, and other communication-disabled individuals would know the route to be traveled by a vehicle and when to get off. Bus systems and other mass transit programs continued to require wheelchair users to be accompanied by another person and to present a medical certificate stating that they were permitted to travel.

The Rehabilitation Act of 1973 (P. L. 93–112), as amended in 1974, created, twelve years after the publication of the ANSI standards and five years after these standards became law, an Architectural and Transportation Barriers Compliance Board (ATBCB) which was authorized to enforce compliance with the standards and with transportation accessibility requirements. Again, expectations that finally something would be done were dashed. The Congress made its intentions clear: the board was to have the authorization to enforce accessibility. And it awarded the board appropriations to do this. Yet the administration chose not to use much of the appropriation. Since its inception the board has been operating on a shoestring budget, concentrating largely upon development of regulations, public hearings, and voluntary compliance efforts. Much greater funding is needed before more effective and comprehensive compliance will occur. Early in 1977 the ATBCB issued regulations governing the compliance process and established, nine years after the passage of the Architectural Barriers Act, a mechanism for its implementation.

The regulations provide for each federal agency involved in architectural and transportation programs to implement accessibility policies under the guidance of the board. This decentralized compliance process allows for programs to be designed for accessibility rather than retrofitted. The board will monitor and assess agency plans with respect to meeting the law's requirements and will examine alternative approaches to overcoming architectural and transportation barriers that already exist.

Both the Department of Transportation (DOT) and the Department of Housing and Urban Development (HUD) play pivotal roles in the removal of barriers, yet both have long traditions of insensitivity to and neglect of the needs of disabled people. One result of this insensitivity is that America today has no national policy on housing and none on transportation for disabled persons. DOT has approached accessibility through a lethargic and tortuous path and has done almost nothing in the way of compliance and enforcement of existing accessi-

bility legislation. The 1973 Federal-Aid Highway Act
(P. L. 93–87) provided for projects funded by the Highway Trust Fund to be accessible, yet DOT declined to enforce these provisions in any comprehensive fashion. In
1974, DOT inaction caused Congress again to stress its
intentions: in P. L. 93–643, it forbade the Secretary of
DOT to approve any project or program that did not
provide for accessibility.

That same year, DOT's Urban Mass Transportation
Administration (UMTA) began reviewing three proto-
types for the TRANSBUS project, a $27 million program
designed to develop "the bus of the future." Two key
issues faced competing bus manufacturers. One was the
accessibility mandate contained in P. L. 93–643. The
other was finding a way to reduce running time, the time
required for a bus to complete its route, thus producing
important savings in labor and equipment costs. Taken
together, the two challenges held the promise of making
bus transportation available to all Americans at lower
rates than would be charged with standard buses. Three
manufacturers rose to the challenge: General Motors, the
dominant force in the industry; the Flxible Company,
GM's major competitor; and AM General, a division of
American Motors that had just entered the busing field.

The three competitors submitted entries and UMTA
studied these in the field as well as in the laboratory.
Then, in May, 1976, the White House announced that
TRANSBUS funds would be withdrawn. Because Flxible
and AM General could not continue in the project without federal support, the announcement effectively declared General Motors the winner. Then in July, UMTA
head Robert E. Patricelli issued "final" regulations for bus

construction which made accessibility optional rather than mandatory. The regulations required only that buses be so designed that a hydraulic lift for wheelchairs may be added. But hydraulic lifts would slow, not speed, running time and would add to the costs of operating bus transportation systems, making it unlikely that local authorities would exercise their option to add the lifts. The regulations are silent on the question of door width, a vital element in accessibility (wheelchair users need a wide door, generally about 3 feet across).

Meanwhile, General Motors announced plans to build buses that would have 30-inch floor heights, down from the current 34–35 inches, and narrow doors. If local authorities decided to purchase and install lifts, the effective floor height would drop to 24 inches. Patricelli's July 27 news conference revealed that UMTA had abandoned the original mandatory 22-inch floor height for an optional 24-inch height—precisely that planned by GM.

Was there collusion between GM and the Executive Branch? Remembering "What's good for General Motors is good for the country," twelve groups of disabled people, including Disabled in Action (DIA) of Pennsylvania, Paralyzed Veterans of America (PVA), and American Coalition of Citizens with Disabilities (ACCD), joined as plaintiffs in a suit filed by the Public Interest Law Center of Philadelphia. Mrs. Sieglinde Shapiro, DIA president, said of the action: "We're not asking for any special place to sit . . . we just want to be able to get on the bus in the first place." The reference was to the struggle in the Sixties to remove the practice in much of the South of placing black riders in the back of the bus. Mrs. Shapiro noted that inaccessible buses were a major factor in undereducation and underemployment of disabled people, and cited statistics showing that accessible buses would increase employment opportunities for disabled people, resulting in a $1.3 billion annual reduction of disability and welfare costs while increasing personal income tax revenues for the federal treasury. The Urban Institute's 1975 study of severely disabled people had concluded that transportation was a major barrier to independent living and employment among disabled people. But the basis for the lawsuit was not in these figures. Rather, it lay in the language of P. L. 93–643 forbidding DOT to approve any project or program that was not accessible and in the earlier accessibility legislation.

A 1976 study by the Stanford Research Institute suggested that it was GM's political pressure on the administration that produced termination of the TRANSBUS program and resulted in the 22-inch floor height being raised to an optional 24 inches. Transit owners and operators, through the American Public Transit Association, also had urged UMTA to alter TRANSBUS standards, fearing the new requirements would mean higher costs. Fortunately, on May 18, 1977, Secretary of Transportation Brock Adams rescinded the Patricelli regulations and required TRANSBUS specifications in all public transit bus designs submitted for federal funding after September 30, 1979. His decision represented a major victory for disabled people.

Subway design is another area in which DOT inaction vitally affects disabled people. The best subway system now in operation (from the point of view of accessibility) is San Francisco's Bay Area Rapid Transit system (BART). When Gallery Place opened its long-awaited elevator in Washington, BART was rivaled by METRO. Despite the fact that UMTA funds were used for BART construction and complete accessibility is therefore required, the system has a number of serious deficiencies. The most critical of these is the fact that access to the stations themselves is severely limited by omnipresent curbs and architectural barriers. Similarly, long passageways between elevators and entrance gates, and between the gates and the train platforms, sizable gaps between platforms and passenger cars that can trap crutches and canes, and the lack of safe waiting places for wheelchair users pose important obstacles. Still, BART is a model of accessibility compared to the older systems in New York, Chicago, and Boston, which are almost totally inaccessible. At a 1974 New York City conference on consumer affairs and disabled people, jointly sponsored by the Mayor's Office for the Handicapped and the city Department of Consumer Affairs, a senior city subway official told the audience that subways "might be accessible by 1995 at the earliest," and told a questioner he was welcome to attend planning meetings at which this might be discussed. "But how can I get to the meetings if transportation and the building both are inaccessible?" responded the questioner, to which the city official had no answer. To date, New York has shown little interest in working on these problems, primarily because of its monstrous financial crisis, a situation Chicago and Boston are also beginning to experience.

The Catch-22 note to urban mass transportation is the reduced-fare provision of P. L. 93–504, the National Mass Transportation Assistance Act of 1974. Despite the fact that most mass transit systems are not accessible, the law requires them to offer reduced fares to disabled and elderly persons. And despite the fact that disabled people most need mass transportation so they can obtain and get to jobs, the reduced fare provision applies only to off-peak hours. A disabled person wishing to take advantage of the reduced fares must first arrange to leave for work very early in the morning (usually before six-thirty) and leave for home early (before three) or to arrive late (about ten) and leave late (after six-thirty)—and then must somehow overcome the barriers to accessibility. This is the program UMTA and the transit systems hail most loudly as evidence of their concern for and interest in disabled people.

The attitude is a common one. In San Francisco, as in Washington, the builders had to be forced to make subways accessible. In both cases, legislation was required. The planning and design had already been completed (in Washington, much of the construction had begun) before the legislation took effect, forcing the designers to go back to their drawing boards at enormous expense in time and dollars. And then throughout the country transit officials used these added costs as justification for not providing accessibility features, ignoring the tremendous difference between planning and retrofitting expenses. Without consulting disabled people themselves, many officials turned psychiatrist and pronounced subways to be "too much" for disabled people because of crowding and jerky motions. The low rate of ridership by disabled people in San Francisco (largely an effect of extra-subway architectural and transportation barriers there) was used, by some convoluted logic, to support this dubious contention. Disabled people, according to these officials, should use the bus. Conveniently ignored was the fact that the buses were inaccessible, including the feeder buses built and operated by the subway officials themselves.

In Atlanta, however, the story is different and may point the way to a more accessible future. Officials there are talking with disabled people, and have done so since before the first bids for a new subway were even received. Efforts are being made to remove barriers outside the stations so disabled people will be able to get to them, as well as to make the proposed system itself accessible. The Metropolitan Atlanta Rapid Transit Authority (MARTA) expects the first stations to open late in 1978 or early in 1979.

Mass transportation, however, is only one piece of the puzzle that is transportation inaccessibility. The Civil Aeronautics Board (CAB) has little to say about accessibility of air travel. The airlines themselves set policy based on CAB tariffs and these policies generally permit pilots to make the final determination about whether a disabled person will be accepted as a passenger. Pilots almost invariably have no experience or training in the area of disability and their decisions may be arbitrary. There is little research evidence available to guide them. An even more basic concern is that no efforts appear to have been made to date to investigate the needs of disabled passengers with respect to designing future aircraft. Thanks largely to the Architectural and Transportation Barriers Compliance Board, airport surveys are being made and improvements in accessibility to terminals have been dramatic, as witness the Tampa and Dallas-Fort Worth airports.

Airport accessibility is an increasingly vital issue as more and more Americans turn to the air for long-distance transportation. The problem is more complex than it might at first appear. P. L. 94–352, the Airport and Airway Development Act Amendments, which became law in July, 1976, presents requirements for accessibility in all new airport terminals and in all renovations begun after the act's effective date. The ideal airport, from the point of view of a traveler who has some kind of mobility limitation (persons in wheelchairs, elderly citizens, mothers with carriages, pregnant women, etc.) and those who have communication problems (blind and deaf individuals, primarily)—would have the following features among others:

• Parking spaces level and at least 12 feet across that are within 200 feet of the terminal entrance;

• Walkways at least 5 feet wide with curb-cuts and ramps at all changes of level;

• Automatic doors level with building entrance, and door handles instead of knobs on all other doors;

• Elevators level with all floors (including garage) that are at least 25 square feet in size and have automatic safety reopening devices and controls no more than 4 feet above the floor and featuring raised letters;

• Transportation within the airport between terminals;

• Vending machines, drinking fountains, telephones, and restrooms designed for use by disabled as well as other persons (low levels, raised letters, etc.);

• Visual and auditory flight announcements, Brailled descriptive information, and teletypewriters (TTYs).

The ATBCB has also been active in making Amtrak more accessible. Although the public railroad corporation's policy since its inception has been to make its facilities accessible, it was only in 1975 that meetings with the board and consumer representatives resulted in action making some of the cars accessible. It is now possible for a person in a wheelchair to travel on an Amtrak train, although only the Amcafe cars are accessible. Efforts have begun to make Amtrak stations accessible as well. The Interstate Commerce Commission (ICC) has specified further changes which are scheduled to be made over the next several years.

ICC has also moved in the area of interstate bus travel. Greyhound now offers a disabled person the option of bringing an attendant at no extra cost; Trailways announced similar policies soon after the Greyhound decision. Problems remain, however, because few efforts have been made or planned for accessibility in stations. As private companies, Greyhound and Trailways are not subject to laws requiring accessibility unless they receive federal subsidies for specific projects.

The 1973 Federal-Aid Highway Act provided funds for alternative transportation systems, such as "Dial-a-Ride" programs offering accessible vehicles for door-to-door service. The problem here is one of cost and segregation. Few disabled people can afford to pay $10 or more (at least) per trip for these services. Even more basic is the issue of segregation versus integration. Dial-a-Ride services take disabled people out of the mainstream, not into it.

Cabs are viable as transportation vehicles, particularly the kind built by the Checker company, but costs are much too high for this to be a realistic alternative for most disabled people. Private cars present another option. The problems here concern insurance and the costs of modifications. Disabled drivers have been shown again and again to have driving records equal to or superior to those of nondisabled persons, yet insurance companies persist in requiring higher premiums for disabled people and their vehicles. The hand controls and other operating alterations that permit many disabled people to drive cost in the hundreds and even in the thousands of dollars. Individuals needing motorized wheelchairs that cannot be collapsed must use vans instead of cars; vans equipped with hydraulic lifts generally cost about $8,000. And special plans must be made for parking so that room will be available for embarking and disembarking from the vehicle.

Coordination in transportation policy is almost entirely lacking. There is no single standard for accessibility of transportation systems that includes provision for the communications problems of deaf, blind, and developmentally disabled persons. Nor is there at present any mechanism for intersystem cross-fertilization and cooperation in this area. Bills are introduced into the Congress and in state legislatures addressing particular problems piecemeal, but these are rarely coordinated or cross-referenced. As a result, a disabled person may be able to make part of a trip but not the entire one; for all practical purposes, the whole trip is impossible. Barriers prevent him from moving from a parking lot to a bus terminal, and from the terminal to a subway station, while other barriers hamper his movement within the lot, terminal, and station.

Housing Barriers

Housing is perhaps the most intensely personal issue involved in architectural and transportation barrier removal. To own a home of one's own is as much a dream for disabled people as it is for other Americans, and even more of a necessity because of inaccessible apartment buildings and the impracticability of making structural modifications there. And the concept of home includes the relaxation of privacy, the enjoyment of prized possessions, the sharing of family togetherness, the memory of highlights from previous years. We may spend as long as a month locating a home or an apartment convenient to work, shopping centers, medical facilities, and schools that is also comfortable, affordable, and an expression of our tastes and values. Then we will spend countless hours arranging and rearranging the furniture and pictures until everything is just right. Each evening as we return from work, the thought of home brings with it a special feeling of comfort and security that makes all the effort worthwhile.

Housing means all this to disabled people—and much more. In a world filled with frustrations and barriers, these people desire a home where they are in control, where things are designed for easy accessibility and comfort, where they may feel safe and secure.

But the dream is an elusive one. Private housing builders have been even more resistant to architectural barrier removal than have been public building designers—and because federal funds figure less frequently in private construction, these builders often are subject to no legal constraints forcing them to build accessible dwellings. The result is that a disabled individual may find it virtually impossible to locate a single accessible home, let alone one that meets all his other expectations—convenience, economics, comfort, taste. In addition to the lengthy search period and the time needed to actually move in, he may need to schedule considerable alterations in the edifice, often at great expense, to make it accessible.

Larry Allison, who has used a wheelchair since he had polio in 1944, has lived in 9 cities and 6 states during the past 33 years—a not unusual pattern of mobility in America today. Yet until one year ago, he was never able to find a single home or apartment that was fully accessible. Testifying at a national hearing on housing needs of disabled adults on June 9, 1975, in Chicago, Allison documented his fruitless search for the unavailable:

When I first came to Montgomery, Alabama, two and a half years ago, the only housing available which was even partially accessible was a retirement center. This is a federally funded project which by federal law should have been constructed to be accessible to people with physical limitations. It was not. . . . I looked at twenty-seven apartments in Montgomery and not a single one would be accessible for a wheelchair without the addition of ramps and structural alterations [which the owners would not permit]. Accordingly, my two and a half years in the retirement center in Montgomery have easily been the most agonizingly humiliating and unhappy years I've ever experienced.

Allison is a successful public relations executive. He built his own home, making it suitable to his needs. All that was necessary was to pour the garage on the same level as the house floor, install wide doors, and lower the medicine cabinet in the bathroom. The special design features did not make the house unattractive to others. In fact, when Allison decided to move to accept a better job elsewhere, he sold his home within two days.

In Chattanooga, Tennessee, a paralyzed woodworker spent four years of weekends putting up his own home, with just a little help from his friends. With a GI pick and shovel, Otis Pickett laid the foundation and then, first sitting on a cushion and later on his wheelchair, placing rocks for the walls and fireplace, built an A-frame home. A woodworker by profession for many years, he installed his own paneling. Friends lifted his chair to the roof and then hoisted him up so he could finish the chimney.

But few disabled people have the necessary financial resources to build their own homes. Severely disabled individuals face an almost totally inaccessible housing market. The single most important piece of federal legislation on housing for disabled persons, the 1974 Housing and Community Development Act (P. L. 93–383), is cruelly inadequate. The Housing Authorization Act of 1976 (P. L. 94–375), extended but did not substantially alter the earlier law. P L. 93–383 authorizes but does not require specialized housing "for the elderly and handicapped." The Department of Housing and Urban Development (HUD) has interpreted the law to mean that massive housing projects that segregate disabled people from the mainstream of American life, where most want to be, and integrate them with elderly individuals in public projects, where few want to be, is the objective rather than accessible housing in the community at large. Protests from consumer groups have begun to produce positive effects upon HUD policy only in the past few years.

Particularly beneficial was Secretary of Housing and Urban Development Patricia Roberts Harris's decision, announced on May 25, 1977, to set aside 5 percent of all new family-unit housing for complete accessibility and to separate in HUD the offices serving disabled people and those focusing upon elderly individuals.

What results from segregation is social isolation. Physical and psychological separation, imprisonment in an institution or in a small, dilapidated apartment building, these are the realities for numerous disabled Americans. The psychic cost is incalculable. Enforced dependency and isolation crush the self-image, and combined with other architectural and transportation barriers may prove devastating. The individual cannot find work because the workplaces are inaccessible, employers discriminate against him, and no suitable transportation is available. Because he cannot find suitable work, he cannot afford decent housing. The barriers are inescapably intertwined.

One issue that is central is that of choice. Disabled people need the same range of alternatives as are available to nondisabled individuals, including single-family homes, group units and transitional housing, and high-rise apartment buildings. Some disabled people are not yet ready for independent living and need the support of group projects while others seek the privacy of single-family units. But most disabled people seek housing in the community, not apart from it. An attractive suggestion is that of adapting existing housing to meet the needs of disabled as well as nondisabled individuals, while building all new units for complete accessibility. The American Institute of Architects and the National Center for a Barrier-Free Environment, both under the leadership of Ted

Noakes, together with the Paralyzed Veterans of America
and the Consortium Concerned with Developmental Disabilities, are advocating integration, not segregation, of
housing for disabled people. The 1974 Housing and
Community Development Act provided funds for rehabilitating existing buildings in its Community Development Program, but the bulk of the funds were allocated
for ghetto areas. Little has been done to date to channel
these funds to integration of housing for disabled people.
The stress continues to be on separate facilities because
HUD regards these as more cost-efficient.

Ultimately, the housing needs of disabled people will
not be met until other obstacles, including transportation
and public building accessibility barriers, are removed as
well. The problems disabled people face in housing are
intimately related to those they face in education, employment, and service delivery. Fragmented programs
that attack one segment of the total array are doomed to
failure. For this reason, a comprehensive, unified approach to the needs of disabled people is urgently
required.

A vehicle now exists through which we can begin to
address these problems. The Rehabilitation Act of 1973
contained provisions in Section 504 stating: "No otherwise qualified individual in the United States . . . shall,
solely by reason of his handicap, be excluded from the
participation in, be denied the benefits of, or be subjected
to discrimination under any program or activity receiving
Federal financial assistance." Following the lead of HEW,
which developed the first set of regulations implementing
Section 504 in the spring of 1977, HUD will prepare a
regulation interpreting the degree to which the protec-

tion offered in the statute applies to housing. The critical component remains that of enforcement: the original (1973) law contained no sanctions for noncompliance, no enforcement procedure, no designated agency responsibility for compliance, and no specific private right of action in the event of discrimination. The potent HEW regulation, however, resolves many of these issues and provides a foundation for vigorous enforcement of the protection offered in the statute, not only in HEW programs, but in all federal departmental and agency financial-assistance programs. It remains to be seen how powerful HUD's enforcement will be, but preliminary signs are promising. Secretary Patricia Roberts Harris initiated important new steps in housing programs for disabled persons immediately upon taking office and has worked closely with disabled people in designing an improved approach which reflects Section 504.

The Right to Live in the World

Architectural and transportation barriers are of the utmost importance because they affect the everyday lives of disabled people. Their presence humiliates these individuals daily, requiring them to seek assistance from others countless times each day with the most basic and mundane tasks. Because of these barriers, disabled people often are unable to handle their affairs independently. The presence of these barriers is a constant reminder to them that they are second-class citizens and the long, hard fight they have had to wage to gain basic human rights reinforces this, telling them that America does not care. These barriers handicap disabled people.

The issue is a central one. If America wants disabled people out of sight and out of mind, it could hardly have done the job more effectively than it has. These barriers form a potent message to disabled people that they are expected to stay in sequestered settings which alone are designed to meet their needs, and that they are not to attempt to integrate into the mainstream of American life. But if America wants to grant disabled people the right to live in the world, it will press vigorously for the prompt and total removal of all barriers. More and more, America is moving in this direction. It has taken enforcement legislation and court decisions, years of advocacy for and by disabled people, and countless confrontations in the communities of this country, but the change is coming. Today, more than fear and prejudice, the issue is turning on economics, and that is a start.

Architectural and transportation modifications often cost considerable sums of money; some reports indicate that it may cost as much as $25,000 to replace a revolving door with one that is accessible to wheelchairs and $15,000 to make a restroom accessible. Actually, accessibility need not always, and in fact seldom does, require radical alterations. Through a concept known alternatively as "reasonable accommodation" and "program accessibility," changes may be made in the site of the work or class, in the procedures used to deliver services, and in other aspects of a company or education program that permit disabled people to gain full equality of opportunity. Mainstream, Inc., a small nonprofit organization in Washington, D.C., estimates that accessibility costs as little as one cent per square foot. A comparative figure Mainstream offers is that it costs an average of 13 cents per square foot just to clean and polish the vinyl asbestos floors found in most offices; this is a continuing, annual cost as opposed to the one-time nature of accessibility costs. Once a facility is made accessible, it serves disabled people without additional expenditure throughout its useful life.

In other cases, initial outlays may be huge. Administrators genuinely concerned about protecting the civil rights of disabled people may balk at spending hundreds of thousands of dollars to do so. The Tax Reform Act of 1976 provides tax relief for businessmen who make alterations for accessibility and some of the costs will undoubtedly come back in the form of increases in patronage by disabled people. And the fact that accessibility serves others than disabled citizens—mothers with baby carriages, for example, and young children—adds to its attractiveness. The fact remains, however, that today America is paying for its ignorance and discrimination during the past two hundred years. Alterations must be made so that all Americans will be able to benefit from programs and facilities subsidized with the tax dollars of working citizens.

For all of this, economics cannot be the issue around which decisions turn. The Supreme Court said long ago that civil rights cannot be abrogated simply because of cost factors. And the courts since that time have consistently upheld this point of view. Disabled people, as much as other people in this country, have rights that cannot be alienated, and these rights include the right to enter into and benefit from programs and services that are publicly supported. To have said, even five years ago, that disabled people could exercise such rights would have been erroneous, but today it is true.

Day by Day

The enormity of architectural and transportation barriers in America today is perhaps best appreciated when the daily problems of disabled people are seen in their infinite minutiae. I know wheelchair users who spend $5,000 annually for taxi services because it is the only way they can get around, who are virtual prisoners in their small apartments, who have been denied jobs because workspaces are inaccessible, who must stay in hotels for months at a time while they seek a place to live, who spend hundreds and even thousands of dollars making an apartment or a house accessible so they can live there.

These barriers affect their ability to get to the corner drugstore, to visit doctors, to move around in their own apartments, to secure assistance in emergencies, to shop efficiently and economically, to gain employment, to visit friends and relatives. The negotiation of a single trip involves a disproportionate amount of planning. First, the determination must be made as to what is accessible and where. This is followed by planning the itinerary with great care, calling a cab or a van, getting out of the house and into the vehicle, getting out of it, securing assistance in hurdling stairs and opening doors, maneuvering through narrow aisles, purchasing an item, reversing the route, securing another vehicle, repeating the process of entering and exiting from it, obtaining entrance again, getting an item, returning, carrying the bags, bringing it all home in time for supper, and paying the exorbitant costs of the trip. Even traffic signals may often be of too short duration to allow a disabled person with severe mobility impairments to successfully traverse the distance between two curbs. The time and expense involved are staggering. And then there are other problems—fear of embarrassment and humiliation, of assault and robbery, of getting lost and being stranded for hours until assistance can be secured. For disabled people who have mobility limitations are in constant danger of unwittingly calling attention to their disabilities. And the possibility of getting lost is quite real for persons who have communication limitations: deaf persons cannot hear departure and arrival announcements and have difficulty talking with others to be sure they are on the right bus or train direction, while blind persons cannot benefit from printed instructions and signs, and mentally retarded persons may become confused with complicated route schedules and the obfuscated language that pervades the transportation system.

We sometimes think of the problem as one of making a building or a vehicle accessible. But architectural and transportation barriers are unavoidably intertwined. Both the building and the vehicle and all points in between must be accessible or the trip cannot be taken. A single trip involves barriers in the building from which you travel, in the route to your destination, in the building you reach, and in the return. All of this must be considered for each trip, the time planned carefully, the costs calculated and the money readied. Multiply all of this by the number of trips required weekly just to survive, let alone those needed to enjoy life, plug in the sacrifices in amenities necessary so that these costs may be paid, add on the time lost from other activities, figure in the intangibles—a cab called that does not come, a building made temporarily inaccessible by renovation—and include the humiliation and anger inevitable at having to do all of this while others enjoy rapid, comfortable, convenient, inexpensive, and vastly more flexible arrangements: that is the day-to-day reality of architectural and transportation barriers.

And that is a major reason for the largely invisible nature of much of the disabled population. Large numbers of these people venture outside the home only once or twice a week, while others are institutionalized, not so much because of their own inabilities as because of architectural and transportation barriers. And participation in the life of the community—attending city council meetings, testifying at public hearings, attending cultural and recreation activities, voting, participating in school events—is sharply curtailed. Wheelchair users are rarely seen on public streets simply because curb-cuts are not provided and most stores have inaccessible doors and stairways, while other transportation barriers may prevent their getting to the neighborhood at all. These barriers restrict not only the disabled individual but his community as well.

Some Next Steps

When we turn from the problems to the solutions, we see once again the interrelated nature of architectural and transportation barriers. The problems and the solutions exist on all levels—federal, state, and local. The solutions must be coordinated and jointly undertaken if America is to become barrier-free.

By far the most important next step is for all Americans to understand the urgency and scope of the problems. There is much individual citizens can do. Many are employees of corporations and organizations that have inaccessible buildings or provide inaccessible services. Pressure from within can be highly effective in removing barriers. Many are voters, and in that role can petition local, state, and federal legislators`and administrators to take appropriate action and can vote down referendums for construction of buildings and transportation systems that have inaccessible features. Many are consumers, and in that role can refuse to patronize buildings and services that are not accessible, while petitioning the owners to make modifications. Many are neighbors, friends, and relatives of disabled people, and in that role can support their efforts to help themselves overcome barriers. Individually and collectively, Americans can work for a barrier-free society. It will take time, decades probably, but much longer without the active involvement of non-disabled private citizens.

ANSI Standards

Under a grant from the Department of Housing and Urban Development, Syracuse University has just finished revising the 1961 accessibility standards originally published by the American National Standards Institute (ANSI), then known as the American National Standards Association. The major reason for the revision is to include housing, which was not part of the original document, and to extend the accessibility requirements to better reflect the needs of disabled Americans who are not in wheelchairs. The original standards, known as ANSI A.117.1-1961, were developed for all buildings and facilities other than private residences, not just for public buildings and not only for new ones. This scope proved ahead of its time and has since been narrowed. The 1968 Architectural Barriers Act, for example, applied only to federally financed public buildings on which construction began after the law became effective. Existing buildings followed regulations only to the extent that federal funding was used. Private buildings were not covered, nor were residences.

The revised ANSI standards are broader. They apply to all buildings and to all renovations, public and private, including residences. They will not, however, have the force of law behind them unless Congress or the administration specifically adopts them for that purpose (HUD is expected to do so, as is the Architectural and Transportation Barriers Compliance Board and the Office for Civil Rights). Legislative or regulative authority is needed for the revised standards, to ensure that they will be vigorously enforced.

The standards must be widely publicized so members of the general public, disabled people, and public and private administrators will become aware of the dimensions of the problem and will know how to direct their efforts. Individual citizens aware of the standards and of the needs of disabled people can observe the extent to which buildings they use meet these standards and can exert pressure accordingly. The standards can be incorporated into local and state ordinances, codes, and laws, providing a uniform requirement of accessibility.

The benefits of an applied and enforced uniform standard are incalculable. Architects and engineers have a ready point of reference for use regardless of where and for whom a building is designed and built. Disabled people can quickly ascertain accessibility of a structure they plan to visit simply by asking if it meets the standard. And compliance efforts are greatly facilitated because a single standard may be used in all instances.

Transportation Standards

No uniform standard such as that of ANSI presently governs the design of transportation vehicles. The Urban Mass Transportation Administration has shown little sensitivity to the needs of disabled persons and has failed to develop standards for accessibility to meet these needs. UMTA action is urgently required because almost all urban mass transportation systems—bus, rapid transit, and commuter railroad—now receive heavy federal financial assistance from DOT. The 1964 Urban Mass Transportation Act made no mention of accessibility. Despite the 1970 Biaggi amendment, UMTA efforts at enforcement have been minimal.

The problem is broader than urban mass transportation, however. Airplane, noncommuter railroad, commercial bus, boat, and automobile transportation are vital to the quality of life of disabled Americans. The Federal-Aid Highway Act of 1973 (P. L. 93–87), as amended (P. L. 93–643), offers an opportunity for such needed improvements as curb-cuts and ramps along streets and intersections. Still, this is far too little.

What is needed now is for a single comprehensive national policy on transportation for disabled people to be designed that includes standards for accessibility, in much the same way the revised ANSI standards apply to construction of buildings. DOT has enormous influence it could, but to date has not, used to effect accessibility. A federal law mandating DOT to develop, implement, and enforce such a standard, together with similar efforts on the state and local levels, would represent a major step forward. Such a standard would coordinate DOT work with that of ANSI and with Section 504 of the Rehabilitation Act of 1973. Private efforts would have to follow public ones for transportation to become accessible for disabled people.

Insurance

The problems with insurance have been discussed briefly earlier in this chapter with reference to transportation. The problems are broader, however, in that insurance companies seldom are willing to offer similar services for similar rates to disabled and nondisabled people, particularly in the areas of home, auto, and health coverage. Individuals with severe health impairments may be unable to secure private health plans. These problems are part of the rationale for the comprehensive health services plans proposed in Congress in 1975 and 1976. Any future such bill must include provisions making it illegal to discriminate against disabled persons by denying coverage or by charging exorbitant rates. Without such protection, many disabled persons cannot be assured of medical care if they leave Medicare and Social Security programs to seek work, and are unfairly penalized for home and car ownership. Disabled people, as much as other Americans, need to be able to select insurance plans they can afford and which meet their needs.

Symbol of Accessibility

In 1969, Rehabilitation International presented a simple design showing a wheelchair as its symbol of access. The symbol has since been widely adopted as a convenient means of indicating accessibility in buildings, facilities, and parking areas. Despite the fact that objections have been raised to the symbol's design—that it shows a wheelchair but not other disability indicators, that it may be seen as a negative rather than as a positive image—the symbol has served a useful purpose. And it is surprising that the facilities it symbolizes are so quickly being used by nondisabled as well as disabled people in preference to less accessible facilities. Ramps, for example, are often used instead of stairs even by those who could use the stairs. Accessible design facilitates travel and use by all kinds of people and this adds to its attractiveness. Anyone who has moved large furniture into an apartment can testify to the barriers posed by steps and narrow doorways, just as anyone who has used a shopping cart can quickly see the benefits of ramped entrances.

Our objective now should be to abolish the symbol of accessibility. America should have no need for it: a barrier-free America would require only a symbol of non-access to designate special-purpose areas that are not accessible. For when only occasional facilities are inaccessible we will have reached our goal.

4

Us and Them

There is a small organization in Boston of people who have paraplegia. Their slogan is "One can make a difference. You." I'm told this is a great conversation starter. Practically no one believes it. The typical response, it seems, is to discount any personal influence and to point to the "rich and powerful" as the only ones who can get things done. But the Massachusetts Association of Paraplegics is right: you can make a difference.

America is becoming so large, so complex, and so fast-moving that its citizens often feel they have lost control. We read the newspapers and watch TV news programs each day, becoming increasingly anxious as we do, and complain to each other about the apparently inexorable isolation we feel from the forces that shape our lives. We tend to forget that legislators are accountable to voters, merchants to customers, school officials to parents.

Yet the fact is that we can make a difference. We have. And we do, each day. For two hundred years, individual citizens have, by acts of commission and omission, built the America we know today. This includes the attitudes toward and treatment of disabled Americans.

Children mocking a disabled child may seriously impair his self-image and weaken his desire to succeed; conversely, acceptance by his peers may make him feel comfortable with them and motivate him to achieve. A disabled adult is affected daily by the attitudes and actions of doormen, salespersons, and passers-by. Seeing a man in a wheelchair trying to open a heavy door, we can hurry by, pretending not to notice; we can show excessive, demeaning pity; or we can, simply and effectively, ask if help is desired, do what is requested, and be on our way. And we can stop a moment and ask why that door is there at all. When we see an escalator, we can inquire if an elevator is available, and if one is not, ask why not. Enough questions, accompanied by subtle reminders that other stores would welcome our business, and sliding doors and elevators may suddenly appear. We can call in on telethons and object to tear-jerker appeals, noting that a more positive tone stressing potential and ability rather than pity and disability might elicit our contributions. And we can go further: at the first signs of plans for a new building, school, or program, we can insist that it be open to and usable by everyone, not only by those of us who are not disabled.

But we rarely do any of these things, partly because we are dubious about our influence, partly because we are unaware of how America handicaps disabled people, and partly because of our attitudes toward disabled people.

Differentness

Attitudes toward disabled people are complex and diverse, reflecting our own differences in background and perception, situational constraints, societal expectations, and variations among disabled people themselves. Yet one central, tragically wrong, assumption seems to pervade most of these attitudes: that disabled people are different from us more than they are like us, that their disabilities somehow set them apart from the rest of us.

Our literature and mass media, from children's books to Shakespeare, from *Frankenstein* to *Psycho,* reinforce this view, achieving the more power because our direct, personal contact with actual people who have disabilities is so limited by architectural and transportation barriers and other obstacles to interaction. Not only are disabled characters in fiction set apart from others but they are often cast as villains plotting demented revenge against pristine heroes or heroines. Physical beauty, in these stories, symbolizes goodness, disability evil. And the evil, disabled ones are always out to destroy the pretty ones. Who has not cursed Captain Hook and cried for Peter Pan and Wendy with every click of the clock? Who did not root for the White Whale against Captain Ahab? Who can remember Quasimodo, the Hunchback of Notre Dame, and not wonder about the intentions of innocent-appearing disabled people? Our memories of these and other characters often become indelible, impervious to any experiences we may have with disabled individuals in real life. Somewhere in the backs of our minds we associate disabilities with sin, evil, and danger.

And pity. Countless films and novels have exploited the problems of disabled people for dramatic effect. In *The Heart Is a Lonely Hunter* a deaf man commits suicide out of loneliness. *See No Evil* revolves around the helplessness of a blind woman pursued by a homicidal maniac. *Tell Me*

That You Love Me, Junie Moon presents a portrait of twisted bodies and minds unable to live in the world. In *Charly* retardation and intellectual brilliance are contrasted in a man who never experiences normality. *A Patch of Blue* draws parallels between blindness and race. The disabled characters in these films often do exhibit strength and autonomy, yet the stress is on the disabilities rather than on the abilities, on difference rather than similarity. Still, nothing in America today so flagrantly play upon our feelings of pity and sorrow as the annual telethons sponsored by various charity groups. These mammoth programs somehow manage to portray disabled children as static, helpless, dependent, lonely, frightened objects requiring our dollars to become human.

Harvey Liebergott, an authority on media and disabilities, believes that current television programming contributes significantly to negative attitudes toward disabled people. The perspective these programs offer, he says,

is always as different from us. Handicapped people are generally portrayed as unique and alone and either dwelling constantly on their deformities or consumed by some sublimating passion that allows them little time for normal human endeavors. When Walt Disney caricatured animals like Dumbo and Bambi and Mickey Mouse, he had them always in family and social situations, growing up, playing, learning, aspiring toward goals that they shared with the rest of society. But handicapped people are always presented as static and dehumanized: they do not grow, or play, or aspire to goals we share, and when they are shown with their families it is always as burdens, not as contributing members.

Yet there is more. The monumental achievements of such disabled people as Beethoven (deafness), Caesar (epilepsy), Franklin Roosevelt (post-polio), and Helen Keller (deaf-blind) have instilled in many of us unrealistic expectations with regard to all disabled people. Deaf persons are expected to be able to lipread almost everything, for example, and those who cannot are thought to be either lazy or stupid. But, with the exception of Helen Keller, these historical figures became disabled after achieving their greatest accomplishments, and all (including Keller) had abilities and drive few of us can match, disabled or not.

Our attitudes are important because they help shape and direct our actions. As long as we believe disabled people are different, we will continue to neglect their needs, placing programs for them lower in priority than services for people seen as more capable and deserving. As long as disabilities engender fear in us, we will continue to treat them in separate, out-of-the-way hospitals and institutions. As long as we pity disabled people, we will continue to see them as objects of charity rather than as equals deserving a say in their own destinies. And as long as the issue is *us* versus *them,* America will continue to handicap disabled people.

Mirrors to the Self

Our attitudes exert powerful and profound effects upon the ways disabled people see themselves. Most of us reach a determination about our intelligence, appearance, productiveness, and intrinsic worth through a process of learning how others see us. Disabled people, of course, are no different. If doctors, therapists, friends, counselors, and family believe a disability will be overcome, the individual probably will come to share this belief. Conversely, if the attitude is that nothing can be done, only a very strong will keeps trying. And falsely high expectations may lead to premature defeat. These attitudes are particularly influential in the hands of those who make critical decisions about a disabled person's life, such as parents, teachers, doctors, and employers, but to some extent the attitudes of casual acquaintances and passersby also have effects, both on the self-image a disabled person is able to maintain and on the quality of his or her life day by day, by affecting the ability to live independently and productively in the community.

Contact and Information

Attitudes appear to be heavily dependent upon contact with and information about what attitudes concern. People who have had extensive contact with disabled people tend to regard them more favorably and to recognize more fully than do people with less contact that they differ greatly among themselves. Similarly, information about disabilities and disabled people tends to make them less fear-inducing. We are uncomfortable about being in situations where we do not know what we should be doing, how we should be feeling, and what we should watch out for. Social psychological research illustrates this. In one oft-repeated study, for example, college students were asked to participate in what was described as a study of reaction to pain. The students were told that while they waited for the experiment to begin, they could sit alone, talk to people who had completed the experiment, or talk to others who were waiting their turns. A surprisingly large proportion chose the last alternative: they wanted to know how others in their situation felt and, by extension, how they should be feeling. Significantly fewer wanted to be with veterans of the study to determine how painful it would be, and still fewer chose to be alone.

This uncertainty may help explain some of our negative attitudes toward disability. We can understand something about blindness, for example, because most of us have at one time or another tried to find our way through a dark room. Deafness is stranger, but some of it we can understand, particularly the simple inability to hear. But cerebral palsy and epilepsy we know little about and these disabilities may frighten us. It is not by coincidence, then, that our attitudes toward blindness tend to be more favorable than those toward cerebral palsy. We know what we can do in the presence of a blind person and thus feel more comfortable there than with someone who is palsied.

Similarly, we have had greater contact, or think we have, with blind people than with persons who have epilepsy. For blindness is instantly visible. Epilepsy, however, like deafness, is not. We do not know a person has epilepsy until he tells us so or an attack occurs; analogously, we are not aware of a person's deafness until we see him signing or hear him talking. Contact is not simply a function of the sheer size of the population: blindness, for instance, is considerably less prevalent than is deafness. Rather, a great deal has to do with our awareness of the disability when we meet disabled people and with the extent to which architectural, transportation, and other barriers impede our contact with them. Moreover, the kinds of contacts we have are extremely important. If we see blind beggars rather than blind lawyers, our attitudes are more likely to be negative. But any kind of contact is probably more helpful than none at all, because it stimulates our interest and concern, provoking us to seek information about the disability.

Attitudes based upon extensive contact and detailed information are resistant to change. But the evidence is that few Americans have had either wide-ranging contacts with or accurate information about disabled people. And this is why there is cause for optimism. Researchers in the field of social psychology have found that attitudes that are products of personal experience and information, as opposed to those which have emerged from secondhand experiences, are deeply held beliefs and feelings people are reluctant to question too closely. One part of this is that attitudes do not stand alone. Rather, they form components of an entire value system developed over a period of years from countless events, many long since forgotten, with innumerable subtle changes along the way. This value system, in turn, has become an integral part of the self-image. To challenge an attitude, then, is often to threaten a complex fabric of beliefs and feelings. And this is why the optimism must be tempered with caution.

The Nature of Attitudes

We usually think of attitudes as having three parts or components: information, emotion, and action. The first, which we might call the knowledge component, concerns how much we know about the objects of our attitudes. Our beliefs, based upon our experiences and information available to us, inform our attitudes. New information which challenges these beliefs produces dissonance, or conflict: we reexamine our knowledge, judge the new against the old, and reach a conclusion about what our opinion should be. This process is important because attitudes rarely change until we have reason to question them, until we are exposed to new and different experiences and information.

The emotional, or feeling, component of attitudes involves what psychologists call "affect." We may be indifferent to someone or something or our feelings may range from intense dislike to mild dislike and from extremely positive emotions to mildly positive feelings. Positive affect tends to accompany complementary beliefs, indifference lack of information, and negative feelings unfavorable opinions. But this is not always true. We may know very little about epilepsy, for example, yet fear it strongly. Analogously, affect and information are not always contingent: we may know a great deal about something yet have little emotional reaction to it, or we may experience feelings independently of the information we have. We may know, for example, that deafness is unrelated to intelligence, yet exhibit anger that a deaf person is attempting to perform a job as difficult as ours.

Attitudes are usually private matters, shared candidly only with close friends and trusted associates. But we cannot always control them and they do guide our behavior in ways we might not desire. We tend to approach objects of favorable attitudes and avoid those to which we have negative attitudes. We act upon the attitudes we hold, sometimes evaluating them on the basis of the results of these actions, and sometimes clinging to them despite indications that we are mistaken in our beliefs or extreme in our emotions.

But there is much more to attitudes than these three components might seem to suggest. People differ genetically in their emotional levels and tolerance of ambiguity, with some more hostile and aggressive, some more impulsive, some more reflective, some more impatient, than others. Genetically determined factors may be rooted in the forebrain, the reticular activating system in the hindbrain, and in the pituitary gland. Temporary illnesses and fluctuations in alertness may also affect attitudes, at least for short periods of time.

Another determinant of attitudes is the situation or circumstance in which the individual finds himself or herself. Attitudes toward a particular disability may change dramatically when someone close becomes disabled. Similarly, attitudes are likely to fluctuate depending upon what it is that is expected: many people report feeling more positively about disabled people when they work together on a project but less favorably when they are in competition. Situational determinants are powerful, so much so in fact that leading educators anticipate widespread attitude change when mainstreaming of disabled children into the public schools becomes an accepted practice and disabled and nondisabled children learn to see each other as individuals.

Attitudes are profoundly influenced by our perceptions of the beliefs and actions of people around us whom we respect and trust. If our friends treat disabled people as equals, we will at least open our minds to the possibility that this may be correct. And social pressure can be a powerful determinant: most of us want to belong, to feel accepted, and for that reason often go along to get along. Children quickly join others in ridiculing disabled children, just as adults join others in avoiding disabled adults.

Attitude Change

The process of attitude change involves a sender, a message, and a receiver. All are important. There is evidence, for example, that we tend to discount messages that are imparted by senders who obviously have a vested interest in our attitudes. We also tend to discount information from individuals whose accuracy we have reason to question. We may attend to an advertisement because we are interested in the celebrity delivering the message, but we may doubt he knows what he is talking about. And we are more likely to be influenced by people who have power over us, such as parents and employers, than by those whose impact is minimal or remote. Characteristics of the source—credibility, attractiveness, influence over our lives, and similarity to us—help determine whether a message will change our attitudes.

Then there is the message itself. As Marshall McLuhan has said, the medium is the message, but this is only partly right. The way something is presented to us—subtly or overtly, authoritatively or hesitantly, passionately or objectively—does make a difference, but so does the message itself. We analyze it, search for logical inconsistencies, and compare it with past information. Fear-inducing messages may cause us to reject them out of hand or to bolster our arguments against them, rather than changing our attitudes, while intellectually oriented messages may reach our beliefs but not change our feelings, and thus prove ineffective as change agents.

Finally, much depends upon ourselves, our past experiences, intelligence, age, anxiety level, and self-esteem, as well as upon how actively we participate in the attitude-change attempt. If we are relatively unacquainted with the subject matter presented and have little immediate interest in or concern with it, attitude change may be swift and dramatic. More intelligent, confident individuals tend to evaluate new information dispassionately more than do less intelligent or less secure persons. Age is relevant largely because, as we become older, we have more and more integration of attitudes into complex value systems, and thus a greater resistance to change. And the degree of our participation is critical. First, attention to the message and its implications is requisite, something very difficult to achieve with young children and very anxious individuals. There is evidence, too, that passive participation leads to less change than does active involvement. Actually experiencing a disability, even though temporary or simulated, can produce dramatic changes.

Thus as long as we are anxious about disabilities and afraid of becoming disabled ourselves, we will resist attitude change toward disabled individuals. Information that first calms our anxieties, then helps us understand the nature of disabilities and the problems they cause, is likely to produce positive changes in attitudes. Analogously, messages that stress the similarities between disabled and nondisabled people, emphasizing the environ-

mental and situational differences, may prove effective.
And opportunities to experience these environmental
barriers—by for example spending some time in a wheelchair—may motivate us to act to remove the obstacles in
our communities.

Attitudes toward disability are often negative because
we fear disabilities, we don't understand them, and we
feel uncomfortable in situations where we experience
fear and uncertainty. Yet these problems can be overcome. Fear can be allayed by offering information that
makes disabilities comprehensible, and uncertainties can
be reduced by helping people understand what they
should and should not do when they are with disabled individuals. Because most Americans have little direct, personal experience with disabilities and little knowledge
about them, it is possible that the attitudes of many persons in America today can be made more positive. This
would mark a major advance toward equality for disabled
persons. Employers who believe disabled people to be inferior often will not even give them a chance to show they
can do a job. Similarly, low expectations by parents and
teachers can defeat a disabled child before he really even
begins. And positive attitudes will affect the environment
itself as we begin to design an America accessible to everyone. Perhaps most important, in a positive social climate, disabled people can assert themselves more freely
than is now possible, striving to achieve to limits defined
not by their disabilities but by their abilities.

Correlates of Attitudes
Toward Disability

Attitudes toward disability exist not in a vacuum but in an entire constellation of other attitudes. The correlates of attitudes toward disabled people, elderly citizens, minority-group members, women, and other groups are important because disabled people are also members of these and numerous other segments of American society. Thus, before we can effect major changes in the attitudes of nondisabled individuals toward disabled people, we will have to consider what other factors are implicated and how these affect attitudes toward disability. And because disabled people vary so greatly among themselves, we need to look at how attitudes toward one disability differ from those toward another.

We have said that America historically has preferred disabled people to be invisible, to be sequestered in secluded settings, to be out of sight and out of mind. But this is also true, to a large extent, of America's attitudes toward poor people, members of racial minorities, and aged individuals. Michael Harrington's *The Other America,* about poor persons, Ralph Ellison's *Invisible Man,* about blacks, and Robert Butler's *Why Survive?* about elderly individuals are vivid accounts of the presence of such attitudes. And these feelings and beliefs are directly relevant to attitudes toward disabled people because the evidence appears to indicate that all are parts of a larger whole: attitudes seem to be generalized, that is, attitudes toward one object tend to be related to and influenced by attitudes toward other objects that are seen as being similar in some way. When these objects are other people, the tendency is even stronger. Persons who exhibit prejudice toward blacks, for example, may also harbor negative attitudes toward elderly, disabled, and impoverished individuals. What this means is that attitudes toward disability cannot be changed effectively in isolation, but are linked inseparably to an entire constellation of societal and individual attitudes toward other groups in America.

The key factor appears to be that of "differentness." The fact of differentness—in age, color, wealth, ability— is there, but so is the degree of differentness. Generally, the more "different" a person is perceived to be, the more negative the attitudes toward him will tend to be. There are exceptions. American blacks are less "different" from white Americans than are black Africans, yet the latter frequently attract more positive attitudes from whites. Despite these kinds of exceptions, attitudes appear to adhere closely to the variable of differentness. An individual usually imposes certain constraints upon his attitudes in order to control his life and be consistent with himself. Thus, he will normally avoid diametrically opposed beliefs about objects he sees as similar because these beliefs would impose a heavy cognitive load upon his mind and make decisions on new situations difficult to reach and to reconcile with his basic values. Rather than judge new situations from scratch, as it were, most people relate them to known circumstances about which they already hold well-established attitudes. This may help explain why some people exhibit little prejudice at all and others express negative attitudes toward almost anyone who is seen as different from themselves and their group.

And it may help explain the remarkably similar reception disabled, elderly, minority-group, and poor people receive in America today. In each instance invisibility has been the rule rather than the exception. In each case prejudice and discrimination keep them that way. In each instance assistance rendered has the flavor of charity rather than of a genuine thrust toward equality. And in each case malnutrition, lack of medical care, inferior education, high underemployment and unemployment, social segregation, and political impotence actually bring these groups together in a tragic and deplorable way.

For disabilities are extremely common among poor people, aged individuals typically are indigent, blacks and other racial minorities have unusually high rates both of disabilities and poverty. Is the price of attitudinal consistency the creation of a separate America of poor, disabled, minority-group, and elderly citizens?

Authoritarianism

The publication in 1950 of Adorno's *The Authoritarian Personality* instigated a turbulence in the social sciences that has yet to calm. The theory this study advanced has become a force in American life, a dynamic change agent that has profoundly influenced conceptions of the nature of prejudice and the roots of discrimination. Briefly, Adorno and his colleagues asserted that an authoritarian would change attitudes based not so much upon the evidence at hand as upon the authority of a power figure. This conceptualization was used to help explain the unquestioning obedience so many Germans gave Hitler in World War II. Whether this explanation is adequate or even accurate need not concern us here; what matters now is the concept of an authoritarian personality as an approach through which to look at attitudes toward disability.

Adorno believed that certain persons were ethnocentric, holding that their ethnic group was superior to others, and antagonistic toward members of other ethnic groups, whose members were thought to have diverse inferior traits and characteristics; politically conservative, bent on preserving the status quo; rigid in their beliefs and unyielding in their opinions when arguing with their peers; and deeply concerned with status, power, and authority. The concept has considerable power in helping us study attitudes toward disabled people. To employ it as such is not to endorse it: I am not saying or implying that any pure types exist who completely ignore any and all evidence and follow only the dictates of an authority. But there are, I believe, people who do have traits we can call authoritarian, and in this sense I believe the concept is helpful.

For the status quo in America today would be very seriously jeopardized by a potent thrust toward equality for disabled, elderly, poor, and minority-group individuals. Persons with a vested interest in things as they are understandably fear such a thrust. We can see this today in the reactions of many men toward women's liberation, just as we continue to see it in many parts of the country to civil rights efforts on behalf of black Americans. We see vestiges of it in the anger of many workers toward welfare recipients.

That is one aspect of the problem. Another is that people tend to judge themselves in relation to others. Rightly or wrongly, they often feel they must be superior to someone in order to have any degree of status in society.

Upward mobility by "inferior" groups threatens this status and produces deep feelings of insecurity. And there is a third aspect. Some people are uncertain of their own knowledge, insecure in their own beliefs, and feel much more confident relying upon and trusting the wisdom of an authority. This is sometimes mixed in with fear of power, so that the safe course appears to be unquestioning obedience to authority.

And there can be no question that in America today disabled people as a group are near the bottom of the social-class ladder. Their emergence as a militant force threatens security and stability, augurs a new era where social position may depend upon a different set of criteria, which threatens those closer to the top. To the trusting authoritarian, there must be a reason for the powers that be to have placed disabled people where they now are, so there they must stay. Many more Americans, however, have deeply ingrained feelings of superiority to persons who are in some way imperfect or who have been relegated for one reason or another to a lower position in society. These feelings have become part of the value systems of numerous individuals, and threats to the feelings may endanger the entire set of values.

The concept of authoritarianism is particularly intriguing as a vehicle for exploring why some people enter fields of work with disabled persons. Adorno proposed that one characteristic of the authoritarian is his need for control over the events òf his life. Teachers and other workers with disabled people may enjoy great amounts of control, while at the same time attracting public admiration for ostensibly being motivated by strong feelings of altruism. Severely disabled children, particularly very young ones, rarely have the capacity to challenge anything their teachers say and do. Deaf children often have little intelligible speech, very limited command of English, and severe experiential limitations. Similarly, young blind children are heavily dependent upon their teachers for information, much of which they must take on faith. A parallel situation exists with many other disabled children. The teacher is master of his workplace (the classroom) more than are most workers and is subject only to periodic supervision from the principal. Theory and practice in special education today are rarely based upon scientific evidence because so little good research has been done on ways to help disabled children learn. As a result of all of this, the special-education teacher enjoys great control. Even if a child should fail, the blame can always be placed with the parents, previous teachers, or the child himself, and with little chance that the teacher's beliefs will be challenged.

Leaders in special education and disabled adults have long discussed the problem of teachers who dominate more than support their children. One reason such teachers are plentiful is that for decades special education had severe personnel shortages. Administrators were at times reduced to taking almost any warm body that was willing to work with the children. Then, too, psychological screening instruments that are sufficiently accurate as to identify authoritarians do not exist. No one knows how many teachers of disabled children are motivated by authoritarian-type needs. The likelihood is, however, that they are relatively few. Most teachers, I believe, from my visits to schools and programs around the country, are genuinely interested in the welfare of their children. Still, the problem is worth our attention. Teachers can do tremendous damage to the self-concepts of disabled children or they can offer enormous encouragement and assistance in the children's efforts to reach their potentials.

Overt and Covert

Attitudes toward disabled people are difficult to measure. The reliability and validity of the scales we have and use are unsatisfactorily low. Another problem is that we can rarely generalize from experimental subjects to disabled people in the population as a whole. A third, equally serious, problem concerns the difference between attitudes people hold and those they express. Robert Kleck's work at Dartmouth has vividly contrasted the two. While most people, slightly over 50 percent in many studies, express attitudes toward disability that are at least mildly positive, almost half express neutral feelings, and few admit negative reactions, Kleck has shown that these may be attitudes people feel they can or should exhibit more than those they actually hold. Overt rejection is socially unacceptable, so most people express neutral or positive attitudes toward disability. Some actually hold such beliefs. Many, however, do not: they are masking their true attitudes.

What Kleck did was to measure physiological reactions—pulse rate, sweating, eye movements, etc.—in subjects who were exposed to disabled people. Despite the fact that many of these people had expressed neutral or positive attitudes, most exhibited considerable discomfort, nervousness, avoidance of eye contact, and other symptoms of negative reactions. Kleck's concern now is to determine how these reactions may be alleviated; that is, how disability may come to be perceived as less fear-inducing by nondisabled individuals. This work is extremely important because fear blocks understanding and acceptance of the needs and desires of disabled individuals, and is a contributing factor in our behavior toward them.

Language

A persistently disturbing aspect of attitudes toward disability concerns the use of adjectives as nouns. In Vietnam, American soldiers called the North Vietnamese enemies "gooks," thus grouping all of them together in a subhuman category, which probably made it easier to kill them without feeling one had violated deeply held ethical convictions about the value of human life. In a somewhat similar, though less drastic way, many people refer to disabled individuals as "the deaf," "the blind," and "mentally ill," as though all deaf people were alike, all blind people similar, and all mentally ill persons identical. That more than a mere quirk of language is involved may be seen in the fact that the adjective-as-noun usage conspicuously deletes the humanizing "people," "person," "individual," and the like. The practice sets disabled people apart from nondisabled individuals and cannot be discounted as of negligible importance. When a disabled salesman of prosthetic devices starts his advertisement with the words, "I've been a handicap all my life," one has to wonder about the effects of adjectives as nouns upon the self-images of people who have disabilities.

Variations on a Theme

Attitudes toward disabled people are not uniform but rather constitute variations on a theme. Sensory disabilities that people in the general public can comprehend are more readily accepted than are many more hidden disabilities. Thus, the visibility of a disability is important as a determinant of attitudes. And visibility, interestingly, seems to be somewhat more related to attitudes of members of the general public than is severity. While epilepsy is rarely a serious problem for an individual who has access to Dilatin, attitudes toward this disability generally are markedly less favorable than those toward blindness. Bearing in mind the methodological obstacles in attitude research discussed earlier, we can conclude that attitudes toward different disabilities appear most to vary according to the extent to which people in general can understand rather than fear the condition. Thus, the loss of a limb has readily understood implications, but few people understand epilepsy and their fear of the unknown translates into negative attitudes.

Mainstreaming As an Attitude-Change Agent

Mainstreaming of disabled children into public schools has dramatic possibilities for attitude change. Instead of some strange, distant "them," disabled children will be seen by other children as real, live, functioning individuals with variations just as bewildering as those of any other group of children. Disabled children will be perceived as people who happen to have specific limitations. It may be that such a view will persist and will continue to inform the children's attitudes as they grow up and become teachers, lawyers, doctors, dentists, salespeople, etc. Teachers and parents have important roles to play in assuring that a climate of relaxed integration occurs, allowing the children to play and study together. For integration only during part of the day (physical education, art, and music, for example) tells children that they are different and unequal in the eyes of their teachers. And parents need to realize that their children will most likely develop strong and healthy self-concepts if they base their perceptions of themselves not on artificial dichotomies between people but upon genuine understanding of themselves and others.

Under grants from the U.S. Office of Education, public television stations in Boston, Massachusetts, and Annandale, Virginia, are producing programs showing disabled and nondisabled children interacting cooperatively in common goal-directed activities. The programs are targeted at nondisabled school children who will have disabled classmates in the 1977–78 academic year. These efforts are the first of their kind, although *Zoom,* produced by WGBH-TV in Boston, has featured disabled children on occasional program segments. What is innovative in the new series is the attempt to show disabled children as natural, normal, children doing things, rather than just talking about their disabilities or standing on display. The message is a subtle one and for that reason may be all the more effective: disabled children are, when all is said and done, children like all children.

The Annandale project, being conducted by WNVT-TV, to take one example, is developing five programs, each half an hour in length, that seek to dispel stereotypes children often have about disabilities. One segment focuses around the efforts of a young blind girl to be allowed to join her classmates on a mountain-climbing trip. In the space of just five minutes, we see a teacher reluctant to assume responsibility for the safety of a disabled child and therefore unwilling to enable the girl to make the trip; an overprotective mother concerned about the ability of her child to take care of herself; the questions of the child's classmates as to what she "sees" on the trip and how she enjoys the view; and the simple struggle of a young girl to live a life of normality. The segment is effective because the blind girl is shown to be an individual with wishes and desires that transcend her disability and because the well-intentioned concerns of those around her are shown to be inhibiting factors. The willingness of one classmate to accompany the blind girl makes her participation on the trip possible: one can make a difference.

Another approach is to integrate information about disabilities into the school curriculum. Discussions about the brain, for example, may easily be extended to explain retardation. Similarly, when children learn about the eye they can experience blindness by blindfolding themselves for part of the day. The objective is to inform the children, to calm their anxieties, and to help them appreciate the problems faced by children and adults who are disabled. Such lessons also help the students learn what to do when they are with a disabled person. The TV programs being produced in Boston and Annandale are designed to be followed by such in-class activities.

Mass Media Approaches

Recent developments suggest that future mass media programming may be more positive about disabilities than previous efforts have been. This is critical because few Americans have direct, personal contact with enough disabled people to be able to form accurate perceptions of them. Thus, television, radio, newspapers, movies, and other media assume added importance. A program like *Ironside*, about a paraplegic police detective, which ignores his disability almost entirely to focus upon his police activities, is a positive influence and serves as one model for future programming. But it is not necessary to gloss over the disability and the adjustments necessary to overcome it. As *Ironside* demonstrates, it is possible to show disabilities and barriers in an unobtrusive manner which may prove to be especially effective in helping to overcome the tendency of many people to see only the disability rather than to focus upon the whole person. Other programs, such as *Eye-Q* (about vision) and *Now Hear This* (about hearing), use a question-and-answer format to focus upon information directly. These shows are effective in helping people overcome their fears about the unknown and are essential for attitude change.

Role Reversal

One successful approach to attitude change is being demonstrated in Boston. There, political figures including judges and congressmen experience disabilities themselves when, on special "awareness days," disabled people offer them simulation training. The approach works because the disabled adults do not stop there: they follow up with meetings designed to begin the process of removing the barriers experienced by the temporarily disabled officials. Role reversal training for personnel officials, in which they play the role of a disabled applicant, may help to eliminate some barriers to employment. Similar training may prove helpful for teachers, therapists, counselors, and others who work with disabled people. Based on the age-old concept of "walk a mile in my shoes," role reversal often produces unexpected insights and lowers resistance to change, even where other approaches have failed.

Beyond Disability

Attitudes toward disabled people revolve, I believe, around the concept of "differentness." But others in America are also perceived as "different," among them elderly, poor, and racial minority group individuals. It is probable that attitudes toward disabled people are inextricably joined, to some extent at least, to those felt toward other groups. For these reasons, it may be that a concerted effort in the schools and mass media channels to stress the essential humanity of all of these persons, to show their similarities to the rest of us, would be effective. In its absence, a separation between "us" and "them" may result in an even more profound division splitting America, leading more and more to the creation of two Americas, depriving this country of the contributions of millions of its citizens, and rapidly reaching the point of no return. Yet, to my knowledge, despite intensive and extensive attitude-change work on behalf of each of these diverse minority groups, no single campaign has been mounted that aims to attack the roots of all of their problems directly by exposing the centrality of the concept of "differentness" and its essential falsity as a guide to interpersonal relations. Differences between people must be valued, not scorned, if America is to be the melting pot it has always claimed to be.

5

No Right to Learn

Katherine Jamieson is in her mid-twenties. For the first twenty years of her life, she was professionally diagnosed as retarded, borderline retarded, and borderline normal, the diagnosis changing over the years as the definition of retardation changed. From the time they first took Katherine to a physician for a diagnosis at age 2, the Jamiesons have filed every report and piece of correspondence they have received and sent. Katherine's story is not unusual, but the file is. And the fact that it is as voluminous as it is means that it provides a rare account of what it means to be disabled in this country.

There are letters to Katherine and long replies. There are pictures she drew, arithmetic problems she tackled. Most of all there are copies of correspondence with "the system"—and the bills, insurance forms, test reports, and rejection slips. For Katherine, despite enormous expenditures of time and money, never did receive an education appropriate to her needs. At 23, she is still at home, unable to hold a job, happy only with her guitar.

There are letters telling the Jamiesons that Katherine will be evaluated, others saying she will not be. There are letters briefly apologizing but firmly refusing even to consider her for admission to publicly supported programs. There are teachers' reports celebrating a small triumph of Katherine's—and many more indicating little or no progress over extended periods of time.

And the tragic fact is that Katherine is not retarded. She has a learning disability. And rather than work with Katherine to find out what would help her learn, most of the educators the Jamiesons consulted said only that there was nothing that could be done (not that they knew of nothing that could be done). And equally tragic is the fact that had Katherine been 2 years old in 1977, the chances that her future would be dramatically different from what it now is are less than even.

Katherine is not alone. An estimated 8 million children and youths aged 3 to 21 are sufficiently disabled as to require special educational services. One million are out of school altogether. Of those in school, only 40 percent are receiving an education designed to meet their needs. More than 125,000 are institutionalized, receiving custodial more than educational services. Perhaps nowhere is our handicapping disabled people more inescapably evident than it is in education.

A Privilege, Not a Right

Education is often thought of as a right, but in fact it has always been a privilege. School officials have always been able to exercise the prerogative of denying admission to and expelling any child they felt did not meet one or more of an often lengthy list of criteria. If a child were thought to be so seriously disabled as to impede the learning of other children or to present problems the classroom teacher was not equipped to handle, the child could be excluded from school. The courts, in fact, upheld this view innumerable times, ruling that a cerebral palsied child who drooled or a student whose clothes or personal appearance were judged unacceptable could be expelled. Nor did a disabled child have a right to an education in his local school district. Despite parental wishes, the child could be remanded to a distant residential school, which in turn could deny admission, again on any number of grounds. Many children, particularly those who were multiply disabled, had nowhere to go except to an institution or back home.

Beginning in 1978, according to the Education for All Handicapped Children Act of 1975 (P. L. 94–142), all of this must change. School systems will be required to adopt a "zero-reject" policy, recognizing the right of the child to an education in a setting most conducive to his or her needs. Then-President Ford signed this landmark legislation on November 29, 1975, but later, when signing the appropriations bill providing funds for its implementation, noted that P. L. 94–142 had raised expectations that could not be met. The appropriations alloted are much lower than Congress had originally envisioned, raising new questions about how comprehensively the law will be implemented and enforced. Will education in fact become a right for the nation's 8 million disabled children and youth, or will it continue to be a privilege?

The answers will emerge gradually. Because P. L. 94–142 mandates a radical change in the delivery of educational services to disabled children, the Office of Education has elected to take an evolutionary approach to enforcing the law. Minimal regulations were proposed on December 30, 1976, which set forth requirements for the initial stages of implementation in the states. The Office of Education expects to amend and extend these minimal regulations on the basis of experience. In an effort to be consistent with the regulations in Section 504 of the Rehabilitation Act of 1973, the Office of Education specifically notes that while P. L. 94–142 is a formula grant program which the states may elect to apply for and receive or alternatively to forego altogether, Section 504 is not similarly optional. Any program which receives federal financial assistance must comply with Section 504 and with its stipulation that no citizen may be denied services or excluded from participation in any program or activity.

Labels

The practice in education has been to find something wrong with a child who does not seem to be progressing adequately in school more than to find something wrong with the instruction being offered. The child is removed from the classroom and subjected to a battery of tests and diagnostic procedures educators themselves admit are generally inadequate, invalid, and unreliable. A disability is "discovered," a label applied, and everyone sighs with relief: "No wonder Johnny wasn't learning. He is learning disabled." And he is learning disabled because he was not learning. The circularity defies reason, but more than that it removes responsibility. The blame for failure now rests entirely with the child.

Once applied, a label is extremely difficult to remove. Teachers, administrators, counselors, and parents now

view Johnny differently. Formerly a child with positive
and unique traits, he now becomes a child with a disability. Compounding the difficulty is the fact that the label
itself is often ill-defined. When Johnny is referred to a
special-education program, the school officials there may
have a dramatically different understanding of the meaning of the label Johnny now bears. The problem would be
worse if the family moved to another state or even to
another town. Yet the label persists. Former U.S. Commissioner of Education James Gallagher called special education for these children "an exclusionary process mas-
querading as a remedial one." Despite the fact that the
label may have been incorrectly applied, only one child in
ten labeled disabled ever returns to a regular classroom.

In 1972 a project on the Classification of Exceptional
Children was set up by the Secretary of Health, Education,
and Welfare to study labeling practices in special education. Its report ("The Futures of Children"), released in
1975, was devastating in its criticism of labels. The project
found that labels were often only vaguely related to the
educational needs of a child. They were applied, charged
the report, more for administrative convenience than for
instructional effectiveness. The entire special-education
system is organized around labels that often ignore individual variations in children and that exclude from services children who do not quite fit into any one of the categorical programs, most notably children who are
multiply disabled, the commission charged, noting that
more than half of all disabled children are now believed
to have more than one disability.

The assumption that underlies labeling is that the categories are meaningful and exclusive: a child who is la-

beled is expected to demonstrate the characteristics associated with that label and not those associated with another label. Thus, a child labeled deaf who also exhibits emotional disturbance may be excluded from a school for deaf children on the grounds that he or she does not meet the characteristics associated with deafness only, and therefore presents problems the school is not equipped to solve, and may be denied entrance to a school for emotionally disturbed children on similar grounds.

Further, labels can become self-fulfilling prophecies. The child labeled mildly retarded receives less instruction lest he be "pushed too hard." Then when he learns less than do others from whom more is demanded, he has "confirmed" the original diagnosis. The process continues and the label grows in impact as the child progresses through school. Eventually he is so far behind that he is removed from the classroom and placed in a class for "slow learners," where again there is a lessening of expectations. In time, he adopts the behavioral patterns of those around him, further "confirming" the diagnosis. All of this, from an original labeling based upon tests that quite possibly were not valid and that measured something other than mental ability (say, reading skill, or alertness, or neatness, or how anxious the child was that day, or the effects of a persistent cold), founded upon a teacher's wish that the child be transferred to another class because he was being disruptive, or based upon any one of a host of other factors unrelated to innate mental ability.

A 1976 investigation by three experts in learning disabilities is illustrative. It is just one of many that could be cited. Two groups of teachers viewed a film showing a fourth-grade boy carrying out various activities. The first group was told that the boy was normal, the second that he was learning disabled. The second group identified significantly more "problems" in the child and less academic potential than did the first group. As the 1975 report of the Project on the Classification of Exceptional Children put it: "To call a child retarded, disturbed, or delinquent reduces our attention to changes in his development. To say that he is visually impaired makes us unappreciative of how well he can see, and how he can be helped to see even better."

Trial and Success

Assessment in special education often focuses upon what a child cannot do well rather than upon what he can do. Instead of looking for what works, we seek indications of what does not. Treatment follows the same pattern. While general educators usually try to strengthen weaknesses as well as enhance strengths, teaching often through the strengths to the weaknesses, special educators tend to dwell upon the weaknesses. Thus, teachers of young deaf children stress maximal use of residual hearing and extended work on speech development more than focusing upon helping the child use his eyes and mind more effectively and teaching academic skills. Through trial and error, the child is helped to reduce the number of errors. I believe this approach is unnecessarily negative, producing undue frustration in the child. Why not focus as much upon trial and success, helping the child to increase the number of successes?

From Diagnosis to Treatment

The process of diagnosis is an extended one, involving a number of steps and a considerable period of time. Neurologist Mark Ozer describes the process this way. Diagnosis begins, usually, with screening. A quickly administered screening device is given to a large number of children by paraprofessionals trained in little more than how to administer the tests given. The idea here is to identify children who may have a problem, without regard for how serious the problem may be. False positives (children identified as having a problem but later shown to be normal) are accepted; the idea is to reduce the number of false negatives (children who have a problem but pass the test). In the next step more highly trained testers administer more sensitive tests designed to discover how serious the problem is and whether the child qualifies for services. This second step typically is performed by psychologists and physicians rather than by educators.

The third step is often for a multidisciplinary "child-study team" to assemble vast quantities of data about the few children identified as having serious problems. Thus, social workers may collate family data, psychologists may administer batteries of intelligence and personality tests, educators may review school records, and medical workers may review the child's health records. Often, a small mountain of data is collected, analyzed, reviewed, and compressed into a single label with educational recommendations accompanying the term.

The child is then referred to a special-education program. Here he is at last placed in a classroom. Much of the child-study team's data is irrelevant to his treatment and is merely filed away. Now, perhaps months after the original screening, an instructional procedure is at last designed. And it reflects as much what the program does and does not have to offer as what the child needs. In fact, the child-study team's findings may be used to justify exclusion or referral to residential programs on the grounds that the child has problems other than those the school is equipped to handle. If this happens, the child's education is further delayed while another referral is arranged.

There are a number of inadequacies with this approach. First, the diagnosis is made not by teachers but by professionals who have very limited contact with a child. The assumption seems to be that the behavior a child exhibits in a test situation reflects something innate, as though the child would perform exactly the same way each time and as though he or she would not change over time. Second, the focus is upon finding something wrong. The child's strengths seem to be ignored in the quest for a label that will describe his or her weakness. Third, the child is seen as a fixed entity who "has" a disability, rather than as a dynamic individual who responds to his or her environment. The process looks for the disability rather than for the ability. Fourth, treatment is postponed until the very end of the process.

Instead, why not examine the child in the classroom in ongoing activity, trying out different strategies to see what works for a given project and communicating results directly to the teacher? The result of such a process would not be a label but rather a prescription for treatment. The child is not removed from the classroom until repeated attempts show that he or she will not respond under the circumstances available in that classroom and requires more "special" intervention. A different classroom with more highly trained teachers and more specialized equipment would then be tried, with the emphasis always upon what can be done to enhance the child's learning and not upon what he or she "has" that is wrong. This process marries treatment to diagnosis, rather than divorcing them. Because a label is not needed, none is used. The focus is upon strengths and how to tap them rather than upon weaknesses and how to label them. We don't sample the problem; rather, we sample the solutions, and choose that which best helps a child learn.

Placement and Treatment

Institutions. Historically, the first programs for teaching disabled children and youth were located in institutional settings. Institutions serve two central purposes. First, they segregate disabled people from the community; and second, they provide convenience for administrators and instructional personnel because children with a given disability are concentrated together and readily accessible. For some children, better educational services may be provided in such settings than in day programs because of the availability of round-the-clock specialized assistance, but for the majority of disabled individuals institutions are probably the least appropriate setting for instruction.

As instruments of segregation, institutions are undeniably effective. Typically located in rural areas, they become small worlds unto themselves. The children are removed from their families for extended periods of time, greatly reducing their visibility in the community and thus public awareness of their needs. Off-grounds excursions are typically highly restricted, both to shelter the community and to avoid criticism of the institution for possible runaways or instances of misconduct.

As vehicles of administrative convenience, they are equally successful. Public school authorities are relieved of the responsibility of providing for children whose needs differ from those of nondisabled children. Similarly, the availability of "special" programs encourages referral of such children and of children who present behavioral or other administrative problems to local school officials. Within the institution operational efficiency is achieved through time-honored mass production techniques, permitting the employment of highly specialized staff, homogeneous grouping of the children, and centralized support services.

As settings for individual growth and development, however, institutions may be the worst possible arrangement. The regulated routines of institutional life depersonalize individuals and deprive them of what is most unique about them—their spontaneity, autonomy, and self-determination. Upon admittance, a child often is fingerprinted, photographed, deprived of personal possessions, and subjected to a lengthy series of tests. From the first day forward, the time of awakening, the scheduling of meals and of classes, and the lights-off period are all regimented with little room for individual preference and variation. Constant contact only with other children with disabilities like his own may produce a disorientation, a false sense of self-worth and of societal expectations, that may prove harmful to the child. Separation from his family greatly reduces its impact upon his sense of values and his identity. The sheltered, specially designed environment discourages the development of essential coping skills the child will need upon discharge into the community. Instead, the child learns patterns of behavior needed in and appropriate to the setting in which he lives, often acquiring traits and characteristics expected of him by his teachers and his peers.

The shock of release into the community at large is often intense. From a sheltered environment where the entire focus was upon adjusting situations to meet his needs and where he was rarely expected to achieve at a level commensurate with that of nondisabled individuals, the youth is now in the community, where the entire focus is on the average and the normal, where he is expected to achieve and perform at a level equal to and even exceeding that of nondisabled persons. Not only has he not been prepared for this, but the community has not been prepared for it either. Suddenly, the youth must shift from a setting where his basic needs were all met by others to a situation where he is now responsible for all of his everyday needs—housing, food, clothing, transportation, daily living expenses, shopping, and employment. The full impact of Handicapping America in all its force descends upon him at once, offering little support or understanding and presenting numerous problems requiring immediate solution.

A teacher of deaf teenagers recounts one instance of limited release into the community which she hoped would help prepare her students for their impending graduation by exposing them to their nonhandicapped peers:

I taught an "honors" English class which consisted of the school's most talented and best-prepared students. As the year proceeded, I became increasingly disturbed by what I felt was a false sense of superiority in these youth. Although they could barely read fourth-grade material, they were so far ahead of the other students in the school that they had acquired a feeling of confidence and assurance I feared would be destroyed mercilessly after graduation. So I planned a visit to a local public high school class whose teacher I knew. When I first mentioned my plans to the students, the silence was, if you will, deafening. I could feel the fear building throughout the room. One student after another asked tentative, probing questions about the class they were to visit: how old were the students, what grade were they in, what books were they reading. Simple, quite normal questions, but revealing their apprehensions.

On the day of the visit, these normally loquacious kids were abnormally catatonic. No one said a thing as we drove to the school. When we entered and stood at the back of the classroom, the kids' bodies were rigid, their eyes filled with fear. I tried repeatedly to get them to say something, even hello, but in vain. They hugged the back wall as though they needed it to stand. Finally, I asked the public school students to come back, talk a little, share their materials, and mingle with my students, but that too was a disaster.

So I gave up and we returned. Still, no one spoke. The next day there were a few questions. The kids seemed to be trying to find defenses they could use to shelter themselves and their egos. They groped for some relieving explanations—perhaps those students were exceptionally bright, older, or very well educated. But they were not; the hearing kids were of normal intelligence, the same age as my kids, and were in an average, not an advanced, English class. Two weeks later, my kids must have found some explanation or perhaps they had forgotten much of what happened, because their exuberance and talkativeness returned undiminished.

This incident is illustrative, I believe, because it shows what even a temporary and very brief exposure to the community can do to students who have been long-term residents in an institution. But when these students graduated, they did not have the option of returning to the institutional shelter. They were on their own.

Despite their inadequacies as educational settings and despite skyrocketing costs, institutions are not likely to vanish from the scene in the foreseeable future. The attitudinal, architectural, and transportation barriers of public schools and local communities will likely prevent many children who should be deinstitutionalized from being referred to local schools. Institutions will continue to play a role, particularly as settings for severely disabled children who have such profound impairments that integration into the mainstream is not feasible, and as centers for research and training. By sponsoring short-term workshops and seminars, institutions can help prepare public school personnel to work with disabled children. Institutions can also serve as resources for diagnosis and evaluation and as short-term placement facilities for children who need intensive treatment before they can return to the public schools. Many institutions have accumulated extremely important reservoirs of skill and experience that will continue to be needed. But the most persuasive argument for their continued existence relates neither to their strengths nor to their weaknesses but to the uncertainty surrounding the current movement toward mainstreaming. Integration of disabled children into public schools may fail for any one or a combination of reasons, including inadequate funding, community resistance, architectural and transportation barriers, and public pressure. Even if it eventually succeeds, mainstreaming cannot be the right answer for all disabled children at all stages in their development. Many are likely to need the kind of specialized assistance available only in highly centralized programs at one point or another during their educational years. And effecting improvements in institutional management and in the kinds of treatment provided are possible and will occur.

Day Programs. Halfway between the institution and total integration is the special day program. Here, the child lives at home but attends a school or class with other children who have similar disabilities. The special day program is administratively convenient, less costly than institutionalization, less disruptive of home life, and thus less likely to produce parental pressure upon the schools than is institutionalization. Compared with total integration, the special day program provides more centralization of specially trained personnel and specially designed facilities and curricula, yet requires more distant transportation for the children, offers less opportunity to mix with nondisabled children, and provides a greater likelihood of labeling and stigma than does total integration. Variations on the special program theme include the resource room, to which the child is assigned for part of the day for intensive assistance, and partial integration, which is an extension of the resource room concept where the child spends a large portion of the school day in a special class unit but is integrated for at least part of the day, usually for recreational, home economics, shop work, art and music activities. Another variation involves the use of an itinerant teacher or consultant, on the theory that it is less expensive to transport the teacher than to move children to a central location. The itinerant teacher after consulting with the classroom teacher helps to overcome particular problems and assists the children individually in special tutoring sessions.

Regular Classes. Despite the availability of institutions and special day programs, a large proportion of disabled children attend regular classes in the public schools. This proportion is likely to increase as a result of the current trend toward mainstreaming. Like institutions and special programs, regular classes have advantages and disadvantages. The teacher may not be prepared to cope with the special needs of disabled students, but this problem can be overcome by appropriate preservice and in-service training and by the provision of consultants and itinerant teachers. The major advantages of placement in regular classes are exposure to realities of competition with nondisabled children, a greater sense of awareness in the community of disabled people's needs and abilities, and a lessened degree of stigma and labeling for the children. These, however, combine with disadvantages that include the possibility that the child may withdraw from too-intense competition and standards he cannot yet meet, the reduced opportunity total integration offers a disabled child of mixing with other children who have similar disabilities (which can be helpful in assisting the child to assess the effects his disability has upon his achievement as opposed to other factors), larger classes than are usually found in special programs and in institutions, and the relative unavailability of specialized assistance and equipment.

Selective Placement. In theory, disabled children are placed where their needs will best be met. In actuality, however, placement is contingent as much upon such factors as sex (males are more likely to be referred out of regular classes into special programs), race (nonwhites are more likely to be placed in special classes), social and economic status (poor children are more likely to be institutionalized or placed in special programs), behavior (disruptive and aggressive actions may trigger referral to special classes), and related factors as upon disability, need, and ability. Even when type and degree of disability are identical, children who are white, middle class, female, and quiet are likely to be retained in regular classrooms while children who are black, lower class, male, and aggressive are referred out. And, equally disturbing, poor children of racial-minority groups often are placed in special classes even when they are not disabled or have mild disabilities requiring only nominal special attention.

Are children in fact better served in special classes, special schools, or institutions equipped with better-trained teachers, more specialized equipment, greater per-capita financial resources, smaller classes, more individualized instruction, and specially designed curricula? The answer, surprisingly, is that we do not know. The available evidence seems to indicate that equal progress is made in regular and in special programs. Research studies evaluating the relative efficacy of regular versus special programs for visually impaired, hearing impaired, emotionally disturbed, mentally retarded, learning disabled, orthopedically impaired, and neurologically disabled children have generally failed to support the intuitively reasonable assumption that special procedures are more effective. The chief advantages of special programs seem to be administrative rather than educational, convenience and community appeasement rather than personal growth. These findings served as a major cornerstone for the mainstreaming movement, buttressing court decisions and leading to P. L. 94–142, the Education for All Handicapped Children Act of 1975.

The Courts of Change

The Education for All Handicapped Children Act did not appear in a vacuum. It followed a lengthy period in which parents went to the courts in efforts to secure for their children the right to an appropriate education. Involved were the equal protection clause of the Fourteenth Amendment, the due process clauses of the Fifth and Fourteenth Amendments, and state constitutions. The most famous case was undoubtedly *PARC* v. *State of Pennsylvania* in which parents affiliated with the Pennsylvania Association for Retarded Children (now Pennsylvania Association for Retarded Citizens) sued the state for failing to provide an education for young retarded children. Thomas Gilhool, the chief attorney for the plaintiffs, was so successful in assembling support from key officials and educational authorities that the state yielded before the court even heard the first day's testimony.

Other cases followed rapidly. Together, they demonstrated five rights that had not previously been recognized: the principles of zero reject, mandatory education, placement in the least restrictive environment, appropriate education, and procedural due process. The first, the principle of zero-reject education, holds that education for disabled children is a right, not a privilege. No child may be excluded from an education merely because he or she is disabled. The second principle, that of mandatory education, complements the first: schools are required to offer equal educational opportunities to disabled and nondisabled children. Thus, an inferior education was ruled unacceptable. Third, the courts determined that disabled children would be most likely to receive an equal educational opportunity in a setting that is as close to that enjoyed by nondisabled children as possible. In other words, remanding a child to a residential school when this is unnecessary is a violation of the law. The principle has come to be called "least restrictive alternative" because institutionalization is held to be highly restrictive, boarding schools more restrictive than day programs, and special programs more so than regular classes. The courts said that a child must be placed in the least restrictive setting in which he would receive an appropriate education. The fourth principle states that the child is entitled to an education appropriate to his particular needs, not just one that meets some of his needs and neglects others. The final principle, that of procedural due process, provides the parents (and the child) with the opportunity to have their wishes known and considered before the child is placed in a program. Nor did the parents stop there. Joined by disabled adults and interested professionals, they fought for and obtained legislation reinforcing these victories.

That the parents of disabled children had to go to court with lawsuits, lobby in the legislatures, and join forces with disabled adults to achieve these basic rights is a sad commentary upon America. Yet the battle is still not won. Appropriations for effecting the newly enacted legislation are, in the opinions of many experts in special education, inadequate to meet the need. Many school systems are resisting the change. In August, 1976, for example, the American Federation of Teachers in its annual convention in Florida stated that it would not accept more than two disabled children per classroom. It is clear that much must be done before disabled children receive the rights to which they are now entitled. Close monitoring of the schools to see that they actually do what is required, training and retraining of teachers-in-training and classroom teachers to equip them to perform in their new roles, test cases to further define what is required by law—these and numerous other steps will be essential.

Mainstreaming

Just what is "mainstreaming"? As was the case with "individualized instruction" a few years ago, no one seems able to come up with a satisfactory definition. Perhaps the 1976 Delegate Assembly of the Council for Exceptional Children (CEC) defined it best. Mainstreaming, CEC decided, is a belief, not a method; a belief

which involves an educational placement procedure and process for exceptional children, based on the conviction that each such child should be educated in the least restrictive environment in which his educational and related needs can be satisfactorily provided. This concept recognizes that exceptional children have a wide range of special educational needs, varying greatly in intensity and duration; that there is a recognized continuum of educational settings, which may, at a given time, be appropriate for an individual child's needs; that to the maximum extent appropriate, exceptional children should be educated with non-exceptional children; and that special classes, separate schooling, or other removal of an exceptional child from education with non-exceptional children should occur only when the intensity of the child's special education and related needs is such that they cannot be satisfied in an environment including non-exceptional children, even with the provision of supplementary aids and services.

Mainstreaming, so defined, is breathtaking in its implications for educational programs. It is also unlikely to become reality for most disabled children for several years to come, unless and until America recognizes disabled people as equals deserving of equal opportunities. But the concept is a sound one and a model for integration of disabled people that can and should be applied to other areas of American life, including housing, transportation, social services, and employment.

Terms: A Note

I have said that a disability is a condition of at least six months' duration that interferes with a person's ability to perform certain major life activities. A handicap, similarly, is an interaction between a disability and a given environment. Yet educators typically call disabled children "handicapped" and "exceptional." It is my belief that the use of the term "handicapped" without reference to the specific set of environmental conditions involved is inaccurate and misleading: it tends to imply that the disability carries equal impact in all settings, which is rarely the case. The term "exceptional," on the other hand, is in my view a euphemism useful chiefly for grouping together two disparate populations—talented and gifted children on the one hand and disabled children on the other. This grouping is purely an administrative convenience, as both categories of children are frequently taught in special programs set apart from the regular classes. I am not entirely happy with the term "disabled" either. It tends to obfuscate the fact that children with disabilities are also children with abilities; indeed, many disabled children are gifted and many are talented. The problem of nomenclature is a complex one in need of further study. It is important because of its connotations as well as its denotations: it carries emotional as well as cognitive baggage. Even if we were to invent an entirely new term, one that had no connotations or denotations *a priori*, its use would soon be curtailed as it inexorably picked up what we strove so mightily to deny it.

Bureau of Education for the Handicapped

The major agency on the federal level responsible for education of disabled children and youth is the Bureau of Education for the Handicapped (BEH). Located in DHEW's Office of Education, the bureau administers P. L. 94–142 and amendments to the original Education of the Handicapped Act. Its Fiscal Year 1977 (FY77) budget of $315 million, while a substantial increase over earlier appropriations, is widely believed to be insufficient for full implementation of the new education legislation. The bureau has made a request for supplemental funding of $200 million for FY77 and anticipates increases that will bring its budget to the $1 billion level by 1982.

Perhaps the best-known program administered by the bureau is the National Information Center for the Handicapped, or, as it is popularly known, "Closer Look." This program sponsors television and other media public-service advertisements urging parents to take a "closer look" at their children to determine if special educational programming may be required. It also serves as a teacher-recruitment vehicle by encouraging people to enter the field of special education. Financed through an annual $500,000 contract, "Closer Look" is remarkably cost-effective. Each year, more than 50,000 parents are reached and helped, at an average cost of just $10 each.

The bureau also sponsors a highly successful program of regional centers for deaf-blind children and youth; a formula grant program providing financial assistance to the states for preschool, elementary, and secondary education for disabled children; research and demonstration studies to find more effective and efficient ways of teaching disabled children; a media program providing captioned films for deaf individuals and offering a special captioned version of the ABC Evening News program over the public television network for the benefit of deaf television viewers; teacher-preparation programs; and regional resource centers offering equipment and consultation to programs serving disabled children and youth.

Despite its success in many areas, the bureau has its share of problems. Responsible for coordinating all Office of Education programs providing services to disabled children, youth, and adults, BEH has had only minimal effect upon other bureaus in the Office of Education. Illustrative is the problem now facing teacher-preparation programs: while the bureau is constituted to prepare specialists in special education, the need now is to prepare generalists in regular education who will be ready to handle mainstreamed disabled children. Similarly, the Bureau of Occupational and Adult Education, which is responsible for vocational education, has only minimal ties with the Bureau of Education for the Handicapped, and this is a major reason for the relative failure of vocational education to provide equal educational services to disabled youth. And the BEH is expected, as the lead agency concerned with educating disabled children, to set an example in affirmative action employment of disabled adults. While some bureau employees on the national level are disabled, few on the regional, special-program, and resource-center levels are, and the bureau has yet to move vigorously to insist upon affirmative action by state and local educational agencies.

Teacher Training

The Office of Education is beginning urgently needed programs for pre-service and in-service training programs for regular classroom teachers who will be responsible for instructing the disabled children mainstreamed under P. L. 94–142 beginning in Fiscal Year 1978. USOE's previous focus upon preparing special-education teachers for placement in institutions and special programs has resulted in what is now a sufficient supply to meet anticipated demands. Indeed, the job market for special-education personnel is now comparable to that in regular education: the supply is actually more than the demand. But today, and for the foreseeable future, most disabled children are and will be spending most or part of the school day in regular classes with teachers who require at least some preparation for handling their needs. The fact that few have benefited fully from such training to date is a major obstacle to complete implementation of P. L. 94–142. The nation's nearly 2 million regular-classroom teachers, as well as several hundred thousand teachers-in-training, urgently need training in work with disabled children. Yet only 9.3 percent of USOE teacher-training funds in the area of education for disabled children is now directed to in-service training of regular-classroom teachers. The proportion must be greatly increased if P. L. 94–142 is to be successfully implemented.

Nowhere is the need more apparent than in the areas of career and vocational education for disabled children and youth. Career education, in the words of Kenneth Hoyt, Associate Commissioner for Career Education at USOE, is "the total effort of public education and the community to help all individuals become familiar with the values of work-oriented society, to integrate these values into their personal value systems, and to implement these values in their lives in such a way that work becomes possible, meaningful, and satisfying to each individual." By contrast, vocational education concerns itself with the development of vocational awareness, attitudes, and skills related to success in particular vocational clusters. Both career education and vocational education are desperately needed if the disabled school-age population is to find employment after graduation.

The need is evident from even a cursory examination of current employment figures and projections for the near future. Research by the Urban Institute, the Rand Corporation, and numerous other university and private research programs indicates that only 42 percent of disabled adults are employed, 63 percent are at or near the poverty level, and 41 percent are considered unemployable. Projections for the immediate future are equally grim. One study has estimated that in the late 1970s only 21 percent of all disabled adults would be fully employed or in college, with 40 percent underemployed and at the poverty level, 26 percent unemployed, and the remainder institutionalized or idle. These current and projected figures represent a massive underutilization of the talents and abilities of disabled people.

Yet career and vocational education are not preparing disabled children and youth with anything even approximating adequate instruction. Educators estimate that 75 percent of physically disabled and 90 percent of mentally disabled youth could work either competitively or in sheltered workshops, yet only 2 percent of all vocational-education students served in 1974–1975 were disabled and the vast majority of these students were placed in inferior, segregated programs. Many of the nation's best career and vocational education programs are architecturally inaccessible, while even more such programs present communication barriers to deaf, blind, and developmentally disabled individuals.

A 1974 HEW-supported study reported that the major

barrier was attitudinal in nature: career and vocational educators lacked sensitivity to the needs and abilities of disabled students and in many instances purposely excluded them from programs designed to impart work-related values and skills. A 1976 General Accounting Office (GAO) survey of vocational-education programs revealed that 78 percent of the school districts studied reported fewer than 20 percent of vocational educators employed to be sufficiently trained in work with disabled students. USOE reported in 1974 that only 500, or less than one half of one percent, of the 266,000 teachers employed in vocational-education programs had received special training in work with disabled students during that year. More recent efforts have brightened the picture somewhat but the vast majority of regular educators working in career and vocational education remain largely unfamiliar with the needs and potentials of disabled students and with techniques of modifying curricula and materials to meet their needs.

The problem is also one of funding. A study begun in 1973 by the Olympus Research Corporation revealed that had the 1968 Amendments to the Vocational Education Act not required a 10 percent set-aside of federal funds for programs serving disabled students, the proportion of such students served would have been even lower than the current bleak figures. In fact, the Olympus study suggested that a substantial number of the states had not even met the mandated 10 percent set-aside requirement, much less matched it with equal state funds. Statistics were unavailable and were in incredible disarray on all levels (local, state, and national), producing an inability on the part of the researchers to determine how many disabled students were being served, what disabilities were represented in the student population, and what services these students were receiving. Because it was administratively more convenient to support segregated programs for disabled students than to allocate funds to mainstream projects, the bulk of the funds spent in vocational education for disabled students was used to finance separate programs in violation of the intent of the 1968 Amendments to spur integration of disabled and nondisabled students.

The Education Amendments of 1976 (P. L. 94–482) call for state and local matching of the 10 percent set-aside federal funds and for integration into regular classes whenever possible. They also require uniform data collection to identify students, programs, staff, facilities, and expenditures, Full implementation is essential, together with coordination of activities with P. L. 94–142 and with Section 504 of the Rehabilitation Act of 1973.

The alternative is stark. For each 100 disabled students graduating from or leaving school annually, the current trend is for 25 to become welfare recipients, 40 to be underemployed, and only 25 to be fully employed or full-time students in higher education, with the remaining 10 either institutionalized or idle. These figures will become more, not less, grim if the current effort is maintained rather than upgraded because of the growing incidence of multiple disabilities and the ever-higher educational requirements for employment.

Institutionalization costs currently average between $5,000 and $7,000 per year per person. With about 600,000 disabled students leaving school each year, institutionalization expenses are astronomical. Full employment, on the other hand, would save this amount and would generate millions each year in income taxes, economy-stimulating purchases, and, most important, the opportunity to earn a living and live a life.

6

No Way to Work

Architectural, transportation, educational, attitudinal, and legal barriers combine with awesome force to deny a majority of disabled adults the opportunity to obtain work commensurate with their abilities and interests. Segregated and inferior educational programs and the inaccessibility of colleges and universities deprive millions of disabled people of the preparation they need to compete with others for well-paying jobs. The same factors are at play when a disabled individual seeks to upgrade his skills to qualify for a promotion. Architectural barriers in places of employment may deny a disabled person entrance, render him unable to perform an activity, or serve as an excuse for an employer unwilling to hire or advance him. All along, the attitudes of family, friends, teachers, counselors, co-workers, and employers tend to discourage upward striving. Transportation barriers may preclude even getting to and from work each day without paying exorbitant taxi or van fares. Under the law (Fair Labor Standards Act) a disabled person may be paid half the minimum wage if these barriers make a sheltered workshop or institutional facility the only source of work he or she can secure.

In America today, according to the best available evidence, only 42 percent of all disabled adults aged 16 to 64 who are not institutionalized are employed. Of those who have severe disabilities, the proportion is about one in ten. Three-fifths of disabled adults of working age are believed to be at or near the poverty level. Nonwhites and women who are disabled are especially likely to be out of the labor force or to report subpoverty level incomes.

The human and social costs of involuntary removal from the world of work are enormous. Yet the federal government apparently prefers to support unemployed disabled individuals rather than rehabilitate them—and the world of work—for employment. Of $21 billion expended annually by 61 federal programs serving severely disabled adults, more than $18 billion goes to income maintenance and less than $2 billion to direct services including training. This, in the face of statistics showing incontrovertibly that rehabilitation doesn't cost, it pays. Estimates of the rate of return from each rehabilitation dollar range from $5 to $70. Even taking the lower figure, the U.S. Treasury would obtain hundreds of millions of dollars annually from taxes paid by disabled adults who are employed. And the amount injected into the economy in purchases by disabled persons able to afford consumer products they previously had to do without would be several multiples of that sum. The reduction and elimination of human suffering and the enhancement in the quality of life for disabled people would be priceless. But there is more.

A disincentive preventing numerous severely disabled

people from even attempting to locate work is the fact that employment automatically disqualifies them from disability insurance and Medicare payments needed to cover high medical expenses. And if the job should be lost through any one or combination of reasons, many beyond the worker's control, these vital payments would not resume for two years following termination of employment. Another disincentive concerns the means test for Supplemental Security Income (SSI). A disabled person able to earn $2,400—$200 a month—would be cut off from all SSI benefits. These benefits are important to help meet often staggering medical costs. It is estimated that a quadruplegic individual would have to earn as much as $12,000 to $18,000 annually to offset the loss of the benefits. Rather than surrender a secure source of support for the vagaries of an uncertain career in a work world full of barriers, a disabled adult may elect not to seek employment. A third factor relates to the high cost of transportation for many severely disabled individuals. While transportation expenses for doctor visits may be deducted from federal income tax returns, transportation to and from work cannot. The result of these disincentives is that to obtain a job a disabled person often must give up important medical and income transfer payments while incurring high transportation costs—and, in all likelihood, the job obtained would be a low-paying, blue-collar one subject to abrupt termination.

The Values of Work

Employment can provide deep personal satisfaction and feelings of self-worth, daily stimulation and challenge, monetary compensation, important fringe benefits, social interaction with a wide variety of people, the opportunity to produce and to create, recreation and enjoyment, and a constant impetus to further personal and professional growth. Enforced idleness, by contrast, denies feelings of self-worth, reduces opportunities for human growth through exposure to new experiences, produces bare subsistence-level living, and may instigate intense feelings of self-hatred and disgust. Underemployment partakes of both of these extremes, imparting some positive rewards while presenting numerous frustrations. Particularly tragic is the fact that employment of disabled people is often a factor not so much of their abilities as of their disabilities. Thus, underemployment of highly gifted and talented individuals may be extremely frustrating and damaging to the individual and his family.

Rehabilitation

The responsibility of preparing disabled youth and adults for gainful employment is, in large part, that of the state-federal vocational rehabilitation (VR) program. The program is administered by the Commissioner of the Rehabilitation Services Administration (RSA) in the Department of Health, Education, and Welfare. All fifty States, the District of Columbia, the Trust Territories, Guam, Puerto Rico, and the Virgin Islands have rehabilitation programs and facilities receiving VR support.

The "rehab" process involves diagnosis and evaluation to determine the extent and vocational implications of the disability(ies), training to enable the person to adjust to and overcome his or her limitations, and preparation for a specific vocation or cluster of vocations. The program is obviously a vital one for disabled people. They do recognize this and respond to it, so much so that expectations are often raised much higher than VR can meet. The program historically has been more receptive to and realistic about the abilities and needs of disabled people than any other state-federal program. Particularly under the leadership of Mary E. Switzer, who was administrator of what was then called the Social and Rehabilitation Service (SRS) during much of the 1960s, VR supported highly significant, trend-setting work in the area of integrating disabled people into the mainstream of American life. It is natural, then, for disabled citizens to turn first to VR for assistance in meeting their needs.

The irony is that, despite its broad mandate, significant progress, and the high expectations of consumers, VR is and always has been a relatively small program. Of all HEW expenditures for severely disabled adults, for example, VR accounts for barely 2 percent. Monroe Berkowitz of the Bureau of Economic Research at Rutgers University, probably the nation's leading authority on economic aspects of disability, did a study in 1974 for HEW that revealed $21 billion in expenditures by the federal government on severely disabled individuals during 1973 exclusive of VR. During that year VR appropriations for services to this population was $375 million.

The argument for a greatly expanded financial base for VR is persuasive. Berkowitz estimated that, in constant 1967 dollars, the annual "cost" of disability in terms of governmental and industry expenditures and wage losses was $35.5 billion in 1970, $51.6 billion in 1973, and was projected to be $222.8 billion by 1990. Taking into account likely continued inflation, the actual cost that year would be $348 billion. These may be conservative figures, striking as they are. Disabled individuals who have not been rehabilitated to their highest potential may depend upon other family members, causing them to forego employment or take part-time work. And, most important, the human costs in enforced idleness, disruption of family life, dependency, and deprivation of an opportunity to contribute to the community are incalculable.

Because of its financial restrictions, the VR program is limited in the number of individuals it can serve each year and in the scope and depth of the assistance available to each client. Individuals who have mental, emotional, and/or physical disabilities and wish to receive VR services must meet a threefold eligibility requirement which encompasses (1) the demonstration, usually through a medical examination, of the existence of a disability, (2) the determination, usually by an individual VR counselor, that this disability constitutes a "substantial handicap to employment," and (3) the expectation, again normally of the counselor, that there is a "reasonable" chance that VR services may enable the person to engage in gainful employment. If the individual is determined to be eligible, an "Individual Written Rehabilitation Program" (IWRP) is prepared by the counselor and the disabled person specifying what services will be provided and in what sequence. The Rehabilitation Act of 1973 (P. L. 93–112), as amended, requires client participation in the preparation of the plan. If the preliminary diagnostic work is not sufficient to enable a determination of eligibility to be made—for example, if the counselor cannot decide whether there is a reasonable expectation of gainful employment—he or she may recommend an extended evaluation of up to 18 months. Termination of services may occur at any time during this period if the counselor determines that vocational potential is lacking or if the client decides to withdraw from the program. An individual who is found ineligible may appeal the decision.

The IWRP is subject to periodic review and revision. It defines the long-range employment goal (mutually agreed to by the client and the counselor) for which the client is being prepared. Intermediate objectives are planned, with approximate target dates for each. The IWRP also specifies the extent to which the client will participate in the costs of services but no needs tests may be applied for the basic services of evaluation, counseling, referral, or job placement. Examples of purchased services include hearing aids, canes, training program services, higher education services, medical treatment and restoration, transportation, readers for blind clients, interpreters for deaf clients, and any other products and services which can reasonably be expected to enhance the client's ability to qualify for and obtain employment. Subsequent to employment, should problems arise, VR is authorized to provide assistance to help the individual maintain employment.

Severely Disabled Individuals

Historically, the tight financial squeeze has forced VR to declare ineligible many severely disabled persons who

would require assistance beyond that VR could offer
without sacrificing services to other clients. In 1973 the
Rehabilitation Act required VR to place top priority upon
meeting the needs of severely disabled clients. Congress
did not, however, substantially increase appropriations so
that these needs might be met. Predictably, then, the total
number of persons rehabilitated each year has declined.
VR is meeting its mandate, however, because the proportion of severely disabled clients to all clients has been rising and is now close to 40 percent. The vast majority of
severely disabled individuals remain to be served and
probably will not be helped until Congress expands considerably its appropriations for VR.

Severely disabled individuals who are not employed
may receive services from programs other than those
provided by VR. Disability not only may prevent an individual from earning a living, it may also result in a loss of
self-confidence, deterioration of basic skills, and dependency upon family members, all of which may produce
disruptions in family life. Disabilities are often accompanied by financial catastrophe, rendering the disabled
person and his family unable to provide for more than
basic human needs. Public services are available to help
resolve some of these problems but, as is the case with
VR, all are restricted in the number of persons who can
be served and in the extent of services available to each
individual. Moreover, vague definitions, conflicting eligibility requirements, and demeaning means tests often
further reduce the number of disabled beneficiaries.

Social services are usually tied to income maintenance
programs. Individuals who desire service must first qualify for the income programs and this may produce

serious problems. Supplemental Security Income (SSI), for example, requires a means test. Direct payments with no restrictions upon use are provided to individuals over the age of 65, blind, or disabled who are below a certain income level. The degree of impairment is not relevant. Thus, an individual who earns more than $200 a month ($400 if blind) is not considered disabled and is terminated from or denied participation in the program. Carried to its logical extreme, which unfortunately is well within the current reality, a deaf-blind paraplegic individual who earns $210 a month is not eligible while a mildly hearing-impaired person earning less than $200 a month is. The problem is compounded because SSI eligibility is a requirement for Aid to Families with Dependent Children (AFDC) and other important federal assistance and service programs.

Perhaps the most serious impediment to disabled people needing social services is the federal support priority for income maintenance programs over direct services. Taking all income programs against all service programs, federal expenditures for the former are ten times that for the latter. It looks as though the federal government prefers to keep disabled people down than help them up. The fact seems to be, however, that administrative and historical factors are more at cause than value judgments. The income programs began long before rehabilitation had demonstrated the capability to assist severely disabled persons obtain employment. Because so many severely disabled persons were declared ineligible for VR services, and partly for that reason were unable to get jobs, they qualified for and received income maintenance benefits.

These reasons aside, the reality remains that today the

federal government spends far too little rehabilitating disabled individuals. We must drastically alter our priorities. Recent research suggests that it is now technologically feasible to train anyone who is alert and has some movement to work. Our resources should be directed to this effort and to finding jobs for the persons helped.

Rehab Group, Inc.: A Success Story

In 1968 a young man named Surhinder S. Dhillon became almost totally paralyzed in an automobile accident. When he applied for VR assistance, he was first declared ineligible because his disabilities were so severe the counselor doubted he could ever work. Dhillon, however, persisted. Finally, impressed with the man's determination, the counselor designed a program to prepare Dhillon for a then rapidly growing field—computer programming.

Four years after the accident Dhillon founded his own company. In grateful acknowledgement to VR for the help it had provided, he named the corporation Rehab Group, Inc. An information sciences enterprise with computer, electronics, travel, and training components, Rehab Group has achieved an annual sales rate exceeding $3 million, employs 250 people, and has become a leader in its field. Dhillon has made it a policy to hire severely disabled persons whenever possible. Currently, almost one-fourth of his employees have severe disabilities. Rehab Group is now expanding into research and demonstration of inexpensive and effective prosthetic devices for disabled people, including wheelchair lifts, vans, and other devices enabling homebound and wheelchair-using persons to receive equality of opportunity in the community. Dhillon, like many of his employees, has little voluntary control over his muscles. A motorized wheelchair enables him to control his speed and direction with the flick of a finger. What he has done, and what thousands like him can do, is to overcome the effects of a severe disability to the point that abilities become operational and effective. Dhillon's abilities count. Today, a corporation president by his early thirties, his greatest frustration is that he cannot locate enough severely disabled individuals whose abilities he needs.

Reasonable Accommodation

The Rehabilitation Act of 1973 introduced the interesting concept of "reasonable accommodation" in employment of disabled individuals. It is not enough for an employer to claim that a disability interferes with a person's ability to perform on a job: the employer must make some alteration in the workspace or in the task itself to remove the obstacles if the applicant is qualified to do the job. Installation of a ramp at the building's entrance may be all that is needed for someone in a wheelchair to obtain and perform a job otherwise inaccessible to him or her. The Tax Reform Act of 1976 encourages this kind of barrier removal by providing an income tax deduction for the employer of up to $25,000 annually.

The concept of reasonable accommodation is not a new one but legislation now requires that it be done and even provides tax breaks to stimulate compliance. Needed now is an extension of the concept to other areas vital to the lives and well-being of disabled people. Severely disabled persons confined for medical reasons to hospitals and institutions may be trained to perform jobs essential for the operation of the facility, becoming, for example, nurses, janitors, and administrators. This is within the capabilities of many such patients. But it is rarely done. One reason involves the attitudes toward the patients of the facility personnel. A second reason concerns the Fair Labor Standards Act provisions allowing such facilities to pay as little as half the minimum wage to their patient-workers, which encourages peonage and discourages professional employment. A third reason relates to the relative failure to disseminate recent research and training developments showing such moves feasible. A fourth reason involves the legislative and program mandates for the facilities which tend to discourage such innovation. None of these, however, is a compelling reason.

On the Verge?

The anti-discrimination provisions of Title V of the Rehabilitation Act of 1973, recent research findings and technology developments, the Tax Reform Act of 1976, a brightening economy gradually emerging from the stagnation of the early 1970s, architectural and transportation barrier removal legislation, the growing militancy of disabled adults, the Education for All Handicapped Children Act of 1975, and growing public resistance to welfare payments all appear to signal that we are on the verge of significantly enhancing employment opportunities for disabled people.

Yet, in all likelihood, progress will be slow. The dominant factor remains attitudes toward disabled people, and all available evidence suggests that these have not changed greatly and are not likely to change quickly. Legislation can accomplish only so much. Ways have always been found to escape legal responsibilities toward disabled people and the probability is that this will continue to be true. Disabled people will not achieve substantially greater employment until America is ready to treat them as equals deserving of that opportunity.

Employer Attitudes

The attitudes of employers toward disabled persons traditionally have been considered the greatest obstacle faced by these people and their counselors and teachers. And the evidence accumulated by a large number of research studies suggests that this is probably correct. The problem, as we have said, has been that employers tend to see, and judge, disabled applicants more on the basis of disability than ability. James Colbert did a survey in Los Angeles in 1973 revealing that employer attitudes toward disabled persons were less favorable than those toward any other prospective group of applicants surveyed, including elderly individuals, minority-group members, ex-convicts, and student radicals. A 1972 study by Arthur Williams in Minnesota found that fully 50 percent of the employers surveyed would not consider any blind or mentally disabled person for any job. Virtually all research studies I have seen report a large proportion of employers unwilling to employ disabled people. The findings are particularly alarming when the survey techniques are examined. Almost invariably, employers are given no information about the individuals to be rated other than basic demographic data and even this is usually restricted to a single parameter (type of disability, for example). Rather than hold that judgments are not possible without knowing how well the individual is overcoming his or her disability, what special training the person has obtained, how well motivated he or she is, and other factors, many employers are willing to rate disabled people on the basis of disability status alone. The experience of many disabled job seekers bears this out.

A number of studies included probes asking why the employer made the ratings he or she did. The results are revealing. Most often cited as reasons for low ratings are cost-related factors. Employers tend to perceive disabled persons as more expensive to hire, train, place, and provide supportive services for than other workers. Other factors involve a perceived lack of flexibility and ability to adapt to changed conditions and new responsibilities on the part of disabled individuals. Less important to the employer are concerns about productivity and absenteeism; the strong records of employed disabled persons in these areas have been stressed by rehabilitation counselors and teachers for several decades as reasons to "Hire the Handicapped: It's Good Business." Two interpretations are possible here. One is that productivity and absenteeism are in fact of less concern to employers. The other is that employers unwilling to hire disabled people, yet aware of the long campaign by counselors and teachers, discount these factors to justify their attitudes. It is encouraging to note that when employers who have hired disabled people are compared to those who have not, the attitudes of the former are dramatically more favorable. While much of the difference may be causal (employers with better attitudes are more likely to hire disabled people) some of the difference in ratings may represent positive experiences with disabled workers.

Negative attitudes among employers influence employment by disabled people in more ways than mere hiring. Also affected are the level of the job in which the person is placed, the compensation awarded, the opportunities for advancement, and the likelihood of being among the first fired in an economic downturn. Available research evidence strongly suggests that when disabled people are hired it is usually in low-level jobs at minimal compensation that are subject to abrupt termination. Employers indicating a willingness to hire disabled people present a substantially greater resistance to promoting them. Again, all of these findings are results of research studies that asked employers to make ratings based upon the disability alone. But what little information is available on actual employment records of disabled people (the Bureau of Labor Statistics does not include breakdowns by disability in its reports, nor do many other labor-force participation surveys) leaves no doubt that most disabled workers have low-level jobs.

During World War II the massive mobilization effort required on the home front and the wholesale enlistment of adult males in the armed forces placed tremendous strains upon domestic industries. They were literally forced to employ disabled persons at all levels and in all job categories. This period represents the only occasion in our history that equality of employment opportunity was ever made available to disabled people. While three decades have passed since that time and numerous changes have occurred, the wartime experience of employers with disabled workers remains a rich source of direct experiential evidence bearing upon the central question of employers: Can disabled people in fact work as well as nondisabled individuals?

Fortunately, a study that is both valid and reliable was conducted shortly after V-J Day by the Department of Labor (DOL) on this question. It is one of the tragic ironies facing disabled people that no comprehensive survey of their performance in employment that has been done since comes anywhere near the standards achieved by DOL in its study, *The Performance of Physically Impaired Workers in Manufacturing Industries* (1948). What DOL did was to compile actual employment records of 11,000 disabled and 18,000 carefully matched nondisabled workers in manufacturing firms across the country. Matching was achieved on sex, age, occupation, plant, shift, and particular job within a plant and on a shift. The results? No significant differences were found between disabled and nondisabled workers on productivity, injuries sustained on the job, absenteeism rates, and voluntary resignation. The only significant difference was for involuntary termination: as the war ended, disabled workers were discharged and nondisabled employees retained. (A "significant" difference, in statistical terms, is one that is unlikely to be a product of chance alone, but in all probability represents the effect of one or more causal factors at work.)

The Secondary Labor Market

Available evidence on the employment patterns of disabled workers indicates that most are in what economists call the "secondary labor market." Basically, this is the hourly wage and seasonal-employment area which is characterized by subsistence-level pay, low-level skill requirements, extremely high turnover, few opportunities for advancement, and a large proportion of part-time and part-year jobs. Economist Thomas Vietorisz of the New School for Social Research in New York City notes that these jobs are often characterized by intentional turnover geared to maximizing employer profit by reducing expenses of maintaining employee morale and granting pay increases to long-term employees. Most such jobs are manual in nature and may be learned quickly (often in as few as fifteen minutes), making turnover feasible as a source of profit rather than loss.

David Tausig prepared a paper for the Urban Institute's Comprehensive Needs study in 1975, analyzing the labor-market participation of disabled individuals who had been rehabilitated by VR in 1970. He found that 51.6 percent of these successfully rehabilitated individuals were in the lowest four occupations studied, while an additional 18.1 percent were in "tertiary labor market" positions—homemakers, unpaid household workers, or sheltered workshop employees—below even secondary-level occupations. Half of the disabled individuals studied earned less than $3,500 annually. The irony is that education and vocational training often are not necessary for many secondary and tertiary labor-market jobs. Yet that is where two out of three rehabilitants were placed after

extensive evaluation, training, and employment counseling. The major factor appears to be employer attitudes.

"Hire the Handicapped" Week

The first "Hire the Handicapped" week was held in 1947.
It was believed at the time to have resulted in the placement of several thousand disabled persons, largely because of the recent wartime experience of employers with
disabled workers. Since that time, several millions of dollars have been expended in the annual program, which
has adopted the slogans "Ability, not disability, counts"
and "Hire the Handicapped: It's Good Business." The
objective is to change employer attitudes. Has the program worked? Can employer attitudes be changed by intensive public relations campaigns? Although no defini-
tive studies have been made on the question, the answer
appears to be no: I have seen no evidence that such campaigns produce marked changes in employer attitudes.
Some examples of research on the question help explain
the resistance of employers to such campaigns.

Sands and Zalkind conducted a particularly well-plan-
ned, intensive, and imaginative campaign to alter employer attitudes toward epileptic individuals in one city
while a comparable city was studied as a control. Both cities suffered at the time from a tight labor supply—they
had few more applicants than were needed to fill available jobs. Despite this fact, only 25 percent of the employers surveyed in the two cities indicated a willingness
to consider hiring applicants with epilepsy. For one full
year Sands and Zalkind conducted a multi-media educational and public relations effort in the experimental city.

Radio appeals were made, newspaper stories arranged, a feature film about epilepsy shown in neighborhood theaters, letters and brochures mailed to employers, and personal visits by church and civic leaders made to personnel officials. At the conclusion of the year-long effort the employer-attitude questionnaire was again administered in both cities. No significant differences were found.

Public relations campaigns geared to changing employer attitudes typically take an objective approach focusing upon work-related statistics. Available evidence indicates, for example, that disabled workers tend to have lower absenteeism rates than do nondisabled employees, perhaps because disabled individuals value the opportunity to work so highly. And the campaigns have helped employers recognize this fact: studies consistently find them citing statistics on absenteeism as one reason disabled people might deserve employment. But their attitudes do not change. The reason, perhaps, may be that employer resistance to hiring disabled people is as emotional as it is cognitive. Or, to put it more bluntly, they are prejudiced. If this is true, they are little different from many other Americans. What makes their prejudice so important, however, is that they control the jobs. Another factor is perceived cost: employers often believe that they must spend more on a disabled than on a nondisabled worker. They may be right. Or then again they may be wrong. The fact is that since 1948 we have accumulated virtually no research evidence on the question that is worth talking about.

What, then, might change employer attitudes? The best and most effective agent of attitude change would seem to be actual experience employing disabled people. By hiring, orienting, placing, supervising, and interacting with disabled persons, employers seem to come to see them as individuals with strengths and weaknesses. Problems that emerge are shown to have solutions, often at little or no cost. The National Association of the Deaf (NAD) recognizes this. Its slogan is "Deaf workers are good workers. Have you tried one?" At the National Technical Institute for the Deaf (NTID) in Rochester, New York, an internship program is part of the curriculum. The rate at which students placed in a company are then hired by that company is high. NTID, in fact, has an annual placement rate of its graduates exceeding 90 percent. In Minnesota, the Technical-Vocational Institute (TVI) program for deaf students reports a similar placement rate. The experience is not unique to deafness. It is general. Employers who experience the problems, as opposed to perceiving them or hearing about them, often change their attitudes.

Public Service Work Programs

Even the most severely disabled individual who is reasonably alert and has some degree of mobility can be helped to perform a job which is both socially useful and potentially gainful for the person. This is the reality today, thanks largely to recent research and to space-age spin-offs of the NASA moon program. Disabled individuals may be trained to perform such necessary work as employers may require with relatively little extra investment of time and money. The ideal is for private industry, competitive, and primary labor-market employment to be

secured. Failing this, public service employment perform-
ing such tasks as microfilming agency records, serving as
readers and interpreters for blind and deaf persons,
helping in the schools as teachers' aides, computer programming and data analysis for compliance agencies, and
similar jobs may be found.

Full employment is a major objective of labor leaders
as well as those who work with disabled people. But it is
unlikely to occur without public service work programs
subsidized by the federal government, such as President Carter's recently introduced job-creation program.
While some such programs specifically serve disabled
persons—notably that for blind vendors under the
Randolph-Sheppard Act and that of the U.S. Postal Service for deaf distribution clerks—few are in existence in
the states and localities where government is growing fastest. Public sector work programs fill a need and should
be expanded. Their major drawback is that they do little
to stimulate the private sector to greater employment of
disabled people.

Another alternative is to take the beginning provided
by the Tax Reform Act of 1976 one step further. While
the act allows up to $25,000 in income tax deductions for
employers making alterations necessary for the employment of disabled people, an additional incentive, this one
for the individual disabled person himself or herself, may
prove highly productive. Just as industry must accommodate in the workspace to permit some disabled persons to
work, so too these persons must make investments in renovating their homes and cars to permit them to work and
must give up important insurance benefits from Medicare
and Social Security when they take a job. A simple change

in medical-support regulations permitting the payments to continue after employment would be a major boost for many disabled individuals.

If it is "reasonable" to expect employers to make accommodations, is it any less reasonable to permit disabled people to continue to receive needed health services so that their take-home pay may be applied to living as well as to surviving? Few severely disabled persons can expect to earn enough to subsidize expensive health equipment and care services and this is a major disincentive to their seeking employment.

If America is committed to employment of disabled people, it will find ways. The technology is here. All that is lacking is the will. In Great Britain each disabled individual is registered with the government when the disability had persisted for at least one year. Every firm in the country is required to allot 3 percent of its positions to disabled workers who are registered before it may hire unregistered persons. Equal pay for equal work is required. But this is coercive. It should be possible for American industry to do better on a voluntary basis.

7

To Right the Wrongs

The human and civil rights disabled Americans seek today are monumental in their simplicity. The right to treatment. The right to education. The right to work. The right to due process. The right to access to public transportation. The right to marry and to bear children. The right to vote. The right to reside in the community. The right, that is, to earn a living and live a life, to be different and to have that difference respected, to receive what they need and give what they can, as free men and women in a free society.

They do not seek the right to be equal. They are equal. What they do want is for the rest of America to recognize this supremely basic fact and to act accordingly. The stark reality is that we do not and the results are chilling:

• In Philadelphia a 20-year-old mother had to go to court for the right to keep her 5-month-old daughter. The city welfare department had attempted to take the baby from her mother on the grounds that the woman had to use artificial limbs because of a birth defect.

• The federal minimum wage for most of the 57.4 million workers covered under the Fair Labor Standards Act is double that required for disabled persons employed in sheltered workshops because of discrimination, architectural and transportation barriers, and educational deficiencies, all of which are beyond the workers' control.

• In Ohio it is illegal for persons with epilepsy to drive. In Florida and Minnesota epileptic youth and adults must submit to case-by-case reviews to obtain drivers' licenses, despite the fact that modern medication in most instances controls the condition.

• The Air Traffic Conference's policy on transportation of disabled people includes the following statement: "Persons who have malodorous conditions, gross disfigurement, or other unpleasant characteristics so unusual as to offend fellow passengers should not be transported by any member" (of the Conference).

• The city of Chicago recently repealed an "ugly law," similar versions of which remain in force in Columbus (Ohio) and Omaha (Nebraska). The Chicago statute read: "No person who is diseased, maimed, mutilated or in any way deformed so as to be an unsightly or disgusting object or improper person to be allowed in or on the public ways or other public places in this city, shall therein or thereon expose himself to public view."

• In California a deaf couple had to go to court for the right to adopt a child. The judge ruled in their favor only because the mother demonstrated she was not mute.

• Disabled foreigners are prohibited to immigrate into this country. Exceptions are rare.

• At least 17 states have had statutes prohibiting marriage by persons who have epilepsy and double that number proscribe marriage of mentally retarded individuals.

How, in the last quarter of the twentieth century in the freest and most advanced civilization the world has ever known, can a minority numbering in the millions be denied basic human and civil rights? The answer seems to come in three parts. First and most fundamentally, America historically has feared and sought to hide disabled people. Some remnants from the witch-hunts of an earlier era are still with us. Second, the disabled people of this country have only begun to unite and organize to obtain and protect basic rights in the last ten years. Democracy in America today seems to mean less that all people are treated as equals than that all have an equal right to demand equal treatment. Disabled people are just beginning to demand that right. The last but still important reason is that few lawyers in America today have the expertise needed to bring cases on behalf of disabled individuals and few disabled persons can assemble the resources to litigate.

Where There's a Will

The resistance of many nondisabled individuals to equality of treatment for disabled people sometimes takes strange forms.

• In Los Angeles the city Board of Public Works Commissioners has liberally interpreted state laws (a rarity) and has insisted that whenever new curbs are built or existing curbs removed, curb-cuts permitting people in wheelchairs accessibility must be made. But public works administrators have found a way around the commission's ruling. Instead of ripping up curbs to install lightposts and traffic signals, as had always been done, they devised an elaborate (and expensive) procedure of digging to within a few inches of the curb, tunneling under it, and installing wires and surface equipment on the street side.

• In San Francisco an architectural barriers law requires new buildings and facilities to be accessible. Within weeks of its passage, a city administrator decided that the word "facilities" did not include sidewalks. Because building accessibility is pointless unless entrance is assured, disabled people returned to the State legislature to have the word "sidewalks" specifically placed in the statute. Said one administrator to disabled advocates: "You bastards are paranoid. What do you want me to do, level the seven hills?"

• In order to keep disabled children out of the public schools (sparing themselves parental wrath) and to avoid the expense of complying with architectural barriers laws, many school districts bus disabled children as many as 70 miles one way to "special" schools. The children must arise as early as 5:00 A.M. and do not return home until after 6:00 P.M. The legality of such action is now suspect as a result of Section 504 of the Rehabilitation Act of 1973 and the Education for All Handicapped Children Act of 1975, but its practicality was always dubious: busing is usually several times as expensive as is most architectural modification and represents a continuing as opposed to a one-time expense.

• Employers seeking to deny disabled people jobs and promotions have resorted to various stratagems. One is to select a candidate and subsequently publicize a job description the candidate (but few others) meets. Another is to employ an obviously unqualified disabled person who is then found incompetent and fired, permitting the company to hire an able-bodied individual.

Too Little, Too Late?

The capacity of disabled people to respond quickly and effectively to adverse decisions and social forces has been sadly lacking in the past. Its emergence in the late 1970's represents a hopeful signal of better times ahead for disabled people. But is it too little too late? The typical situation historically has been for disabled people to become aware of a building's inaccessibility only after the structure has been largely or completely built and of a program's inaccessibility after it has been designed and inaugurated. The retrofitting costs are so enormous at that point that community resistance is united against the renovations disabled people request. Had disabled people been active politically in the early 1900s, for example, it is entirely possible that much of America would now be accessible to and usable by disabled as well as nondisabled people.

Why have disabled persons been slow to organize? Clearly, the fault does not lie entirely with them. The powerful social forces behind institutionalization are partly responsible because segregation of disabled people removed them from community awareness. Then again, poor educational services have been a contributing factor. It is only the politically sophisticated, highly educated citizen who has the necessary knowledge and confidence to lead a successful advocacy effort. Poverty enforced by educational deficiencies, employer discrimination, and other factors have also contributed: it is necessary to attend to immediate, personal needs before one can turn to larger social issues. Transportation and communication barriers have also kept disabled people isolated from each other, reducing their opportunities for united action.

Services for disabled individuals were confined almost entirely to institutions until the turn of the twentieth century. Then, with World War I focusing attention upon the needs of returning veterans who had become disabled, services for disabled people began to move more and more into the community. At the same time, disabled individuals began to come together more frequently, often for recreational and social purposes, but increasingly for discussion of the problems they shared. Special education expanded rapidly during the period between the two World Wars and better education enabled more disabled people to assume positions of responsibility in the community. Then, during World War II, thousands of disabled people replaced able-bodied workers who had been called into service. Given an opportunity to work, these disabled people responded with important contributions to the mobilization effort, keeping American industry productive. After the war, however, they were displaced by returning veterans and this spurred many disabled individuals to turn to increased social activism. National organizations were formed and expanded representing virtually all categories of disability. The protests of black Americans in the 1960s and of women in the early 1970s incited higher expectations from disabled people. In 1974 a group of 150 leaders formed the American Coalition of Citizens with Disabilities which was to serve as an umbrella organization bringing together the different, single-disability organizations that had emerged. But by that time, much of America had already been built. It may have been too little, too late.

Inaccessible Counsel

Very few private attorneys in America have either the technical knowledge or the willingness to bring cases on behalf of disabled people. One factor is the relative obscurity and frequent absence of legislative precedents upon which to base a case: disabled people have rarely been involved in litigation until very recently. A second factor is the almost universal lack of training in law schools concerning issues basic to the civil rights of disabled individuals. A third factor is the high cost of legal research in areas where judicial precedent is not widely known. Mass transit or architectural barrier suits, for example, require hundreds of hours and thousands of dollars' worth of legal research, including extensive interviews with engineers, architects, and authorities on disability. The lack of judicial precedent means that appeal all the way to the Supreme Court is a distinct possibility and this alone can discourage plaintiffs.

Thomas Gilhool, the attorney who headed the *PARC* v. *State of Pennsylvania* suit and now directs the Public Interest Law Center of Philadelphia, a major source of legal expertise in education and transportation for disabled individuals, has proposed a simple and elegant solution to this problem. Gilhool's plan calls for coalitions of organizations of and for disabled people to support statewide teams of lawyers which would bring suits on cases perceived as important precedent-setting efforts. An equally appealing alternative is for a central coordinating team of lawyers and paraprofessionals who have worked in disability to provide legal-research support for lawyers selected by disabled individuals to represent them in court. This plan would enable any disabled individual to choose his own lawyer while encouraging attorneys to accept such cases. Little will be accomplished, however, until law schools provide instruction on issues central to the civil rights of disabled people and raise the consciousness of law students to these issues.

Legal Precedents

Despite formidable obstacles, considerable progress has been made over the past ten years, both in the courts and in the legislatures. The courts have affirmed a right to liberty, treatment, education, just compensation, voting, and transportation. Legislation on architectural barrier removal, civil rights, education, housing, and transportation has been at least as important.

The Right to Liberty

O'Connor v. *Donaldson (U.S.L.W. 4929)*. On June 26, 1975, the U.S. Supreme Court ruled that a state cannot confine involuntarily an individual who is not dangerous to himself or to others. In the unanimous opinon, Justice Stewart rejected the concept that a community may exile an individual whose presence it finds disturbing: "May the state fence in the harmlessly mentally ill solely to save its citizens from exposure to those whose ways are different? . . . Mere public intolerance or animosity cannot constitutionally justify the deprivation of . . . physical liberty." The plaintiff had been confined to a mental hospital for fourteen and one half years during which time he had received little more than custodial care.

The Right to Treatment

Wyatt v. *Hardin* (*M.D. Ala. 1971, 325 F. Supp. 781*). On March 12, 1971, Judge Johnson held that patients involuntarily committed to an Alabama hospital were being denied the constitutional right to "receive such individual treatment as (would) give each of them a realistic opportunity to be cured or to improve his or her mental condition." The case is particularly important because it resulted in a definable set of standards for treatment.

The Right to Education

Mills v. *Board of Education of the District of Columbia* (*U.S. District Court, D.C., 1972, 348 F. Supp. 866,878*). On August 1, 1972, Judge Waddy ruled that ". . . requiring parents to attend school under pain of criminal penalties presupposes that an educational opportunity will be available to the children. The Board of Education is required to make such opportunity available." The judge found that separate educational programs violated the right of due process of a group of children alleged to have mental, physical, and emotional disabilities and that the D.C. Code, which requires parents to enroll their children in school and which provides criminal penalties for failure to do so, implies the right of the children to be so enrolled. Judge Waddy also held that lack of funds was insufficient basis for denial of education: "If sufficient funds are not available to finance all of the services and programs that are needed and desirable in the system, then the available funds must be expended equitably in such a manner that no child is entirely excluded from a publicly supported education consistent with his needs and ability to benefit therefrom." Summing up his opinion, the judge ruled: ". . . that no child eligible for a publicly supported education in the District of Columbia shall be excluded from a regular school assignment . . . unless such child is provided (a) adequate alternative educational services suited to the child's needs which may include special education or tuition grants, and (b) a constitutionally adequate prior hearing and periodic review of the child's status, progress, and the adequacy of any educational alternative."

The Right to Just Compensation

Souder et al. v. *Brennan et al. (U.S.D.Ct., D.C., 1973, 367 F. Supp. 808).* There is no law guaranteeing disabled people the right to employment. The courts have, however, ruled on the right to fair compensation for work, and the Souder case is a landmark decision in that respect. On November 14, 1973, Judge Robinson ruled that hospital patients performed work that was of economic benefit to the institutions and was therefore subject to remuneration. His now-famous words were: "Economic reality is the test of employment and the reality is that many of the patient-workers perform work for which they are in no way handicapped and from which the institution derives full economic benefit. . . . the economic reality test would indicate an employment relationship rather than mere therapeutic exercise. . . . The fallacy of the argument that the work of patient-workers is therapeutic can be seen in extension to its logical extreme, for the work of most people inside and out of institutions is therapeutic."

The Right to Vote

Caroll et al. v. *Cobb et al. (Superior Ct., N.J., Civil Action No. L-6585-74-P.W.).* On October 29, 1974, the Superior Court of New Jersey ruled that 33 residents of a state school for mentally retarded students were eligible to vote if they could answer all questions asked of potential voters. Subsequent to the decision, the plaintiffs registered to vote and many actually did so in the November 5 election.

The Right to Transportation

Lloyd, et. al. v. *Regional Transportation Authority, et al., 548 F. 2d 1277 (Seventh Circuit Court of Appeals, Illinois).* On January 18, 1977, the Seventh Circuit Court issued an opinion that Section 504 of the Rehabilitation Act of 1973 offers protection to disabled people which they may apply to accessible transportation. The decision is important not only for transportation but for civil rights generally because the court ruled that because Section 504 contains language modeled after Section 601 of the Civil Rights Act of 1964, the Supreme Court's unanimous decision that Section 601 provided a right to private cause of action (the right to go to court with a grievance) meant that the same holds for Section 504. The Supreme Court had ruled in *Lau* v. *Nichols* (414 U.S. 563, 566).

Legislative Loopholes

Important advances have been made in federal legislation protecting the basic human rights of disabled people.

Laws are now on the books concerning architectural accessibility, civil rights, education, housing, and transportation. Yet the langage of the laws, and of the regulations governing their implementation, is more often permissive than mandatory, general than specific, loose than tight. In almost every instance the protective curtain is riddled with loopholes. In large part, implementation and enforcement of these laws will form the battle lines for disabled activists for years to come. The gaps vividly illustrate the compromises made in the legislatures as the needs of disabled people were balanced against the demands of other, more powerful, groups in our society. A sustained advocacy effort will be needed to close the gaps and to obtain for disabled people the rights these laws were originally intended to provide.

Architectural Accessibility

The Architectural Barriers Act of 1968 (P. L. 90-480) applies to any building or facility intended for public use or one which may be used for employment of or residence by disabled people that was constructed, leased, or altered in whole or in part with federal funds after standards for accessibility were promulgated by the Department of Housing and Urban Development (HUD), the Department of Defense (DOD), and the General Services Administration (GSA). The standards were issued in September of 1969 and consisted of the American National Standards Institute (ANSI) specifications prepared in 1961. Specifically excluded from the law are existing public building and facilities not scheduled for renovation with federal funds and military facilities, as well as privately owned residential structures.

The law contained no provision for enforcement and compliance and in fact it never was enforced. HUD never issued its regulations governing housing sections of the law (Title 24, Part 40). P. L. 90–480 became an empty document, devoid of meaning. Five years later, when it was glaringly apparent that compliance was not forthcoming, Congress passed the extraordinarily influential Rehabilitation Act of 1973 (P. L. 93–112) which, among other things, created the Architectural and Transportation Barriers Compliance Board to enforce architectural accessibility under the law.

The example of Gallery Place has been cited earlier to illustrate the weakness of architectural barriers legislation. The Washington Metropolitan Area Transit Authority (WMATA), which built METRO, was aware several years prior to the passage of P. L. 90–480 in 1968 that modifications in the design of the system would be needed so that all potential passengers would have access. In March, 1970, P. L. 91–205 amended P. L. 90–480 to specifically include the METRO system as being mandated to effect accessibility. On October 23, 1973, the District Court of the District of Columbia issued a permanent injunction halting any further construction that did not provide for accessibility. Rather than comply, the builders went back to court in October of 1976 seeking a waiver so that its stations could be opened even if they did not have elevators. On December 14, the waiver was granted contingent upon installation of elevators by July 1, 1977. The elevator was in place by that time.

What Gallery Place showed is that neither P. L. 90–480 nor P. L. 91–205 had sufficient enforcement authority to require compliance. Disabled people were forced to go to court. Another, equally instructive, example is provided by transportation accessibility legislation. Five separate laws require all public transit vehicles, buses in particular, to be as fully accessible to the mobility disabled and elderly populations as the state of their development will permit. The TRANSBUS research supported by the Department of Transportation demonstrated that only the wide-door, low-floor, ramped bus would provide accessibility and that such accessibility was in fact technically and economically feasible. Only that bus would meet the needs of 13.3 million Americans who are handicapped by high floors and steps in buses, 7 million of them elderly and 6 million disabled. Despite clear congressional mandates, five times repeated, the Department of Transportation bowed to General Motors and accepted its design for a bus which does not significantly improve accessibility and which in addition adds to rather than cuts running time, meaning that it would cost almost twice as much to operate in urban areas as the accessible bus. Again, disabled people were forced to go to court. Twelve organizations sued for a reversal of the DOT decision. The case was dropped following Secretary Adams' TRANSBUS decision.

The Architectural and Transportation Barriers Compliance Board, established by Section 502 of the Rehabilitation Act of 1973, has the potential to enforce architectural and transportation accessibility legislation. Yet here, too, the law contains debilitating loopholes. The board, which has representation from nine federal agencies, is expected to ensure compliance with standards developed by these very agencies. In effect, the agencies are monitoring themselves, a classic conflict-of-interest situation. The board itself has no statutory standard-making authority. A second weakness is that the board has no line-item status in the federal budget. Rather, HEW allocates general department-wide funds for the board. The fact that the board must compete for funds is largely responsible for its chronic lack of resources: it is currently functioning on only half of its congressional appropriation. A third weakness is that while the original language contemplated placement of the board in the office of the undersecretary of HEW, the version that became law put it in the office of an assistant secretary in the department. For an agency that is supposed to have authority across government, location in an assistant secretary's office in a single department makes its work nearly impossible.

The board is authorized to withhold funds from any building or facility found not to be in compliance with standards. And it has successfully resolved more than 100 of the 450 complaints it has received, almost all through amicable discussion. It has also held numerous public hearings focusing public attention upon the barriers it seeks to remove and it has worked cooperatively with Amtrak officials to make trains more accessible and with the FAA to make airports accessible. It has done this on a budget of less than $600,000 and a staff of eleven (seven of them professionals). Despite these successes, it seems clear that the board will have to be elevated out of its present location, probably to the Office of the President or to the Office of Management and Budget, provided with line-item status in the federal budget, and granted standard-making and compliance powers before its work can be done properly.

On October 18, 1976, President Ford signed into law amendments to the Architectural Barriers Act of 1968. P. L. 94–541 substitutes mandatory language for the much more permissive wording of the earlier legislation. The Administrator of GSA, the Secretary of HUD, and the Postmaster General were given unambiguous mandates to prescribe design standards for accessibility in their respective jurisdictions and to establish a system of continuing surveys to ensure that compliance with these standards is obtained. P. L. 94–541 also expands the scope of covered buildings by specifically including privately owned buildings leased to the federal government for public housing and other purposes.

The Tax Reform Act of 1976 contains, in Section 2122, provisions for tax relief for businessmen who make renovations to remove barriers to disabled employees, applicants, and customers in any facility or public transportation vehicle. Beginning on January 1, 1977, a maximum deduction of $25,000 per year is permitted, with most costs depreciated over the useful life of the property. No such provisions apply, however, to disabled people who make similar modifications to ensure that they will be able to get to and from work and to perform in their jobs.

Civil Rights

The Rehabilitation Act of 1973 (P. L. 93–112) contains, in Title V, historic legislation establishing basic civil rights for disabled people. Section 501 forbids discrimination against applicants and employees of the federal government solely on the grounds of disability. Section 502 establishes the Architectural and Transportation Barriers Compliance Board. Section 503 requires nondiscrimination and affirmative action by federal contractors and subcontractors (primarily private businesses) on behalf of disabled applicants and employees. Section 504 offers the greatest protection of the four sections and comes closest to granting disabled people the rights accorded members of racial, religious, and nationality minority groups by the Civil Rights Act of 1964. Title V is so important that it deserves a detailed analysis.

One of the most disturbing aspects of Title V is that the original law (P. L. 93–112) was passed without any public hearings on these four sections. There was no distinct legislative history from which program administrators could gauge the intent of Congress. This deficiency was partially remedied by the inclusion of hearings specifically on Title V in the 1974 Amendments to P. L. 93–112. It became clear during these hearings that Congress intended for regulations to be issued on Section 504, a matter that had been subject of considerable debate, and that it was the desire of Congress that the civil rights provisions of Title V be enforced.

Section 501 concerns nondiscrimination against applicants and employees in federal government solely on the basis of disability. Implementation is coordinated by an Interagency Committee located in the Civil Service Commission. No sanctions are included in the law, nor is any complaint procedure outlined. The Interagency Committee can encourage agencies to comply (by, for example, publishing lists of agencies in compliance) but has no recourse against noncomplying agencies. Each agency is expected to develop its own affirmative action plan, but not all have done so. There are no regulations governing Section 501, nor does the Civil Service Commission wish to issue such regulations. Another problem is that many of the "selective placement coordinators" (individuals responsible for helping disabled people obtain employment in federal government) are not trained in disability. There is no remedy of back pay for an applicant who has been discriminated against, although the person may use the regular Commission appeals procedure with his or her grievance; this procedure is, however, time-consuming, cumbersome, and provides for no appeal past the agency's decision.

Section 502, which established the Architectural and Transportation Barriers Compliance Board, built into the board three damaging restrictions. First, it provided no line-item status for the board. Second, it located the board within the office of a single department's assistant secretary, from which position it cannot conduct government-wide enforcement. And third, it constituted the board of the heads of nine federal agencies—the departments of Labor; Housing and Urban Development; Transportation; Health, Education and Welfare; Interior; and Defense; and the General Services Administration, Veterans Administration, and U.S. Postal Service—without granting the board itself standard-making or compliance powers. Thus, the board is charged with somehow enforcing the law upon the very agencies of which it is composed, while power to design and enforce standards rests, not with the board, but with the agencies.

Section 503, which is concerned with affirmative action by private enterprise contracting with the federal government, has had limited success in its first few years but is at present the most effectively enforced of the four sections. There is little investigative outreach to locate noncompliance instances. Rather, the burden rests upon the individual to file a complaint. The Department of Labor's Office of Federal Contract Compliance Programs, which is responsible for implementing Section 503, attempts to resolve complaints through arbitration and amicable discussion. It has the power to withhold federal funds in the event of noncompliance, but it has yet to do so. Some of the cases require as much as 18 months to resolve, but most are closed within 90 days. Some examples:

A Virginia resident who had been diagnosed as mentally ill but who had controlled the condition successfully for two years with medication prescribed by a psychiatrist was fired by an electric equipment testing company after an examination of health records convinced the employer that continued employment would lead to undue pressure. The individual was rehired in an equivalent position at equal pay after the Department of Labor intervened. Back pay was also awarded.

•

A Florida resident who was blind in one eye left employment with the understanding that upon completion of college studies reinstatement would occur. However, the individual later decided against continuing higher education and applied for reinstatement as a pipe layer. The company refused. When the Department of Labor investigated, the individual was awarded back pay, seniority was restored, and reinstatement occurred.

●

A woman from Georgia was awarded almost $6,000 in back pay after she was summarily fired from her position with a railroad company which believed her visual impairment prevented her from working satisfactorily. Upon investigation, it was found that she qualified for the position and could in fact perform her work. She was rehired.

●

A deaf man in Chicago was fired when a company official decided that the impairment prevented him from lifting heavy equipment at the company plant. He was rehired.

●

A woman living in Texas was fired because of a speech impediment. The bottling company for which she worked offered her back pay totaling $3,000 and her position plus lost seniority after the Department of Labor investigated. The woman accepted the back pay, but because she had already accepted a position with another company, declined the job offer.

These cases, while only five of those successfully negotiated, show that discrimination can be found and remedied. The need now is for the Department of Labor to expand its work into industry surveys designed to identify covered contractors which are not complying with the law. The present system places too much emphasis upon complaints, thus rendering assistance only to those so-phisticated few who are aware of their rights and know how to obtain them.

It is Section 504, however, that contains the greatest promise. The words are bold and starkly simple: "No otherwise qualified handicapped individual in the United States . . . shall, solely by reason of his handicap, be ex-luded from participation in, be denied the benefits of, or be subjected to discrimination under any program or activity receiving Federal financial assistance." Virtually every area of modern American life is inexorably intertwined with federal financial assistance and this is why the protection Section 504 offers is so important. It offers the one unifying key to mainstreaming of the disabled population into the general community on all fronts in a cohesive and orderly manner. The promise, however, must be tempered by reality. The provisions of Section 504 affect virtually every department and agency in the federal government. Accordingly, each agency must develop its own set of regulations implementing the protection for disabled persons granted in the law. These regulations are sure to differ widely in the degree to which they offer genuine and enforced protection against discrimination on the basis of disability. Nevertheless, Section 504 is historic in its scope and depth, the single most important civil rights provision ever enacted on behalf of disabled citizens in this country. As such, it deserves an extended discussion and analysis.

The Rehabilitation Act of 1973 was twice vetoed by then-President Richard Nixon. It became law on September 26, 1973, when Nixon signed a revision passed by one of the largest majorities any piece of legislation has

ever attracted. Frustrated in his attempts to deny enactment, Nixon was in no hurry to implement the law, particularly the potentially explosive Section 504. For 31
months, virtually nothing happened. Then, soon after
Gerald Ford decided to campaign for the position he
held by appointment and aware that action on Section
504 might increase his chances of election, Ford issued an
Executive Order assigning responsibility for coordination
of Section 504 implementation to the Department of
Health, Education, and Welfare and specifically to the
Office for Civil Rights. Soon thereafter, the Office held a
series of meetings with representatives of organizations of
and for disabled people to discuss basic issues relating to
the scope and purpose of Section 504. On May 5, 1976,
the Senate held oversight hearings to determine why no
regulation had been prepared and why no enforcement
activities had begun. The Senate's intensive questioning
of the Office's staff members made clear its intention that
a regulation be issued promptly.

On May 17, 1976, a "Notice of Intent to Issue Proposed Rules" was published in the *Federal Register*. It contained a series of questions on major policy issues and a
draft of a proposed regulation. The public was given 30
days to comment on the questions and the proposed regulation. This was one of the first times such a step had
been taken by any federal agency; the first step normally
is to issue proposed regulations and invite comments,
rather than to issue an "intent to" which requests comments. More than 120 written comments were received
during this brief period. HEW also held ten well-at-
tended public hearings throughout the nation. On July
16, a proposed regulation appeared in the *Federal Regis-*

ter. This time the public was given 60 days to comment. More than a thousand comments were received; 22 more public hearings were held. All told, more consumers, recipients of federal assistance, and other concerned individuals and organizations participated in the process than had been the case with any other regulation affecting disabled people.

Following this intensive and extensive period of debate, HEW developed and revised the regulation until, late in December, a draft that appeared to satisfy both the Secretary and the staff was produced. The draft was considered "final" but it was never signed. On January 14, 1977, then-Secretary David Mathews decided to send the regulation to the Congress for comment. This unprecedented step, particularly in view of its timing—just six days before Mathews was scheduled to leave office—was widely interpreted as yet another delaying mechanism. On January 17 representatives of the Children's Defense Fund and the American Coalition of Citizens with Disabilities met with Mathews in an unsuccessful attempt to dissuade him. The next morning he transmitted the regulation to the Senate and that afternoon the Institute for Public Interest Representation went to court seeking a temporary restraining order forbidding the Secretary to delay signature. The order was granted but was rescinded the next day by a three-judge appeals panel after the Secretary had requested a stay of execution.

When Joseph Califano came into office, disabled people expected rapid promulgation of the regulation. President Jimmy Carter had, in a September 22 press release, denounced the delay by the Ford Administration and had promised more compassion for disabled people:

I oppose discrimination in any form, and when my administration moves against discrimination it will vigorously seek out and redress discrimination against the handicapped. . . . As President, I will take all necessary action, through specific legislation and the appropriate exercise of executive powers, to insure our handicapped citizens equal protection under the law, equal opportunity for education, employment, and other services, and equal access to public accommodations and facilities. . . . No administration that really cared about disabled citizens would spend three years trying to avoid enforcing Section 504.

Disabled individuals and organizations interested in the welfare of disabled people called Secretary Califano's attention to these pledges by the President and urged rapid signature. The Office for Civil Rights itself urged rapid signature. Califano called in several consultants to advise him and they too recommended immediate signature. His general counsel-designate, Peter Libassi, who had directed the Office for Civil Rights under Lyndon Johnson, met with consumer representatives and confidently predicted rapid signature.

Then, in an abrupt about-face reminiscent of David Mathews's last-minute decision to send the regulation to the Hill, Califano named an intradepartmental task force to study the regulation, to see if rewriting into simpler and shorter language was possible and to explore the potential impact of promulgation. Consumer representatives reluctantly accepted the decision and a 30-day review period followed. The task force, co-chaired by Libassi and Assistant Secretary for Human Development Arabella Martinez, spent most of March, 1977, complying with the Secretary's request. In addition to justifying major decisions made on the wording of the regulation by the previous Administration, assessing probable impact upon disabled people and upon recipients of federal financial assistance who would have to comply with the regulation, revising the inflation impact statement to reflect current conditions, and outlining an enforcement plan, the task force was charged with responsibility to develop a "layman's guide" interpreting the regulation for the general public, particularly for those members of the population who because of their disabilities would be most directly affected.

The task force was originally envisioned as a 30-day endeavor. March 19, 1977, would have seen its end; in meetings with Peter Libassi, however, disabled persons and their representatives were told that the review would continue for another several weeks. Particularly disturbing to consumers were indications that the task force was considering major changes in the regulation that would have the effect of drastically weakening the protection promised in the law. In a letter to President Jimmy Carter dated March 18, disabled leaders reviewed the tortuous history of the regulation, discussed the apparent inevitability of significant changes, and proposed the belief that a deadline of April 4 would offer the Secretary sufficient time to complete his review and issue a strong regulation. If he did not act by that date, the letter said, disabled people "would be forced to undertake national political action." Copies of the letter were sent to Califano and Libassi. On March 31, Libassi revealed some of the changes being proposed in the regulation. Some were inconsequential, but several were major and would, disabled leaders believed, have a devastating effect upon the protection offered.

The demonstration took place in Washington, D.C., and nine other cities on April 5, 1977. Over five thousand disabled people were involved, directly or indirectly, in the sit-in and related activities. In Washington, Denver, New York, and San Francisco, the demonstration continued the following day. The San Francisco group would remain for 25 days. For three weeks disabled people not involved in the sit-in visited top White House officials, representatives in the Senate and the Congress, and leading civil rights organizations serving women and minority groups. Thousands of letters, phone calls, and telegrams were sent and made to Califano and to the President. Two vigils at the White House were held to call Carter's attention to HEW's inaction. The demonstration was a direct cause of the decision by Secretary Califano to sign a regulation on April 28, 1977, in advance of his publicly proclaimed May 10 deadline. Equally significant, the regulation he produced protected the rights of disabled people in a courageous, intelligent, creative, and sensitive manner. Disabled people throughout the nation were exhilarated. In San Francisco the sit-in demonstrators embraced. In Washington leaders of major organizations of and for disabled people held a press conference praising the action of the Secretary and held champagne parties in celebration of the event. "This is a historic moment," said one demonstrator. "It marks the first time disabled people across the country came together in large numbers, disregarding the barriers of race, sex, age, disability category, geographical region. It marks, not only the beginning of the end of an era of unjust discrimination but also the inauguration of an era of political strength for the citizens of this country who are disabled. And the protection offered by the regulation is the broadest, most potent ever afforded disabled people. This is truly an occasion for rejoicing."

The demonstration had effects other than its intended result. In Denver newspapers reported that regional-office HEW officials had little choice but to put up with the protesters because "even the jails of Denver are inaccessible." In San Francisco Black Panthers brought food to the sit-in demonstrators from Safeway Stores cooperating in the protest. In Washington prominent Senators and Congressmen who had seldom considered the needs of disabled persons became firm advocates. Top White House aides undertook crash courses on disability. Major unions, recognizing that many of their members become disabled each year, joined the struggle. Church groups supplied food and shelter for demonstrators in Washington and San Francisco. The demonstration and the reasons for it attracted the attention of virtually every major television and radio station in the nation. The protest was front-page news in the newspapers of America's major metropolitan areas. Feature stories illustrating the problems of individual disabled people, and how these problems might be resolved through Section 504, appeared in magazines and newspaper supplements.

The result was a nationwide consciousness raising. Disabled persons learned that "you *can* beat City Hall." Equally important, they learned what their rights were to be under Section 504, information their government had noticeably failed to disseminate adequately. Nondisabled individuals saw, not the dependent children telethons had accustomed them to, but independent, aware, law-abiding, and intelligent individuals who happened to be disabled. And at least some of society's discrimination against disabled people was exposed and understood by many who had never had occasion to consider its impact.

More lasting will be the effects upon the lives of disabled people. The regulation promulgated by Secretary Califano requires all new facilities and buildings constructed with HEW funds to be barrier-free, i.e., readily accessible to and usable by disabled persons. All existing structures must be made accessible; no exceptions are allowed by the regulation. Employers may not refuse to hire disabled applicants if these applicants meet all requirements for employment. Pre-employment physical examinations may not be made, although such tests are permitted in the period between hiring and the start of actual work. Every disabled child and youth in the country is entitled to a free, appropriate, public education in as close a setting to normal as is appropriate for the student; segregation into separate programs and separate facilities solely on the basis of disability is forbidden unless these are shown to be the optimal placements for the child. Educational and other service programs must provide auxiliary aids, such as readers for blind individuals and interpreters for deaf persons, to ensure full participation. And it may be that because public television stations are supported by public funds, educational programs sponsored by HEW must be captioned for the benefit of deaf viewers.

More generally, the regulation states that no recipient of federal funds may deny a disabled person participation in regular programs just because of the fact of disability or because a separate program specifically for disabled people is available. This means that "separate but equal" is rejected for the first time in history as a guideline for serving disabled people. No employment criteria which discriminate against disabled persons and which are not specifically related to performance on a job may be used. Indeed, the regulation uses the term "reasonable accommodation" to describe steps employers are required to take in the event a qualified disabled person is prepared to do a job but some modification of conditions is needed to permit him or her to do so. Thus, if a machine signals malfunction with an auditory alarm, this alone cannot constitute sufficient reason to deny a deaf person employment as a machine operator if he or she is qualified. Rather, the signal may be replaced by or supplemented with a flashing light that would permit the deaf individual to detect malfunctions.

Recipients of federal financial assistance are not required to make every classroom and every facility accessible to disabled people. The basic principle, rather, is that alternatives must be equal in quality and scope. Thus, some classes might be reassigned to other (more accessible) buildings and some work might be relocated to other settings. Similarly, intentional and unnecessary segregation of disabled people from other citizens may not be undertaken; rather, such separation as does occur must take place on an equitable basis that does not discriminate against disabled individuals.

Section 504 is more than a HEW concern, of course. It affects recipients of federal financial assistance whether this assistance comes from HEW or some other agency. Because President Ford's Executive Order 11914, issued on April 28, 1976, assigned lead agency responsibility to HEW for developing the regulations, the other agencies awaited HEW action before beginning development of their own regulations. Most will probably make at least some substantive changes in the HEW version; others will restrict themselves to modifying the wording to fit their own programmatic requirements. And the issue of who enforces the regulations is still not resolved. To have each agency enforce its own regulation is one approach. An interesting alternative, however, and one proposed by President Carter's transition group, is to transfer authority for Section 504 enforcement, along with several other programs serving disabled people (such as the President's Committee on Employment of the Handicapped, the President's Committee on Mental Retardation, the HEW Office for Handicapped Individuals, and the Architectural and Transportation Barriers Compliance Board), to an office in the Executive Office of the President responsible for coordinating all programs and activities affecting disabled people.

Education

Legislation on education has followed litigation in this area and has consolidated advances first made in the courts. Section 504 is, of course, vital to the protection of educational rights for disabled individuals. But the Education for All Handicapped Children Act of 1975 (P. L. 94–142) and the Vocational Education Act Amendments of 1976 (P. L. 94–482), together with earlier legislation, form the cornerstone of equal educational opportunity for disabled people. P. L. 94–142 is so far-reaching in impact, in fact, that the Office of Education spent more than a year writing the regulation governing its implementation. Again, as with Section 504, powerful forces shaped the ultimate direction of the regulation, with many school officials urging weakened language and disabled adults joining with parents to press for strong wording.

Passed by the House in a 404 to 7 vote on November 18, 1975, and by the Senate the following day in an 87 to 7 margin, P. L. 94–142 was signed into law by then-President Ford on November 28. Beginning in 1978, the federal government will contribute to state and local education agencies a fixed proportion of the extra expenses they incur in educating disabled children. In 1978, the proportion will be 5 percent; it will gradually increase to 40 percent by 1982. State and local education agencies are directed to give first priority to children now out of school and second priority to those currently receiving inadequate services. It is estimated that one million disabled children and youth are out of school altogether and that as many as 60 percent may be receiving inappropriate assistance. Each state is required to certify in assurances that extensive child-identification procedures are being undertaken, that all children located will be served, that the due-process right of children and their parents will be respected, that parents and guardians will be consulted prior to placement in an educational program, that individual written educational programs will be prepared and periodically updated for each child, and that children will be educated in the "least restrictive alternative" setting that is appropriate to their needs and abilities.

The Developmentally Disabled Assistance and Bill of Rights Act (P. L. 94–103), enacted in October, 1975, strengthens services and provides safeguards for retarded, cerebral palsied, epileptic, and autistic children, youth, and adults. Education, health, welfare, and rehabilitation services are coordinated under the act so that existing gaps in service provision may be filled and available resources used more efficiently. The rights of developmentally disabled persons to treatment, liberty, and high-quality services are to be assured. Each state is required to institute a "protection and advocacy" program that is independent of any state agency and that has the authority to pursue legal, administrative, and other appropriate remedies to ensure the protection of the rights of developmentally disabled individuals.

Housing

The Housing and Community Development Act of 1974 (P. L. 93–383) provides, for the first time, federal support for alternative living arrangements for disabled persons. While federal legislation since 1941 has made disabled people eligible for inclusion in projects sponsored by the Department of Housing and Urban Development (HUD), only 1,000 dwelling units designed for disabled persons were constructed in the period between 1964 and 1975, with almost none during 1941–1964; by contrast, almost 800,000 units were built for elderly individuals during the 35-year period. From the beginning, housing programs for disabled and elderly individuals have been joined in the same HUD office, despite the insistence of both groups that their needs differed substantially. Moreover, despite the oft-expressed wishes of both groups for private, single-unit dwellings and small group homes,

HUD continues to fund multi-million-dollar projects of 100 to 150 units for "economic efficiency." P. L. 93–383 is important because it establishes funding for other kinds of housing for disabled people, notably group homes and congregate housing (in which central kitchen and dining facilities are shared), for rent-supplement payments, and for special projects aimed at removal of architectural and transportation barriers in the community itself. But it does not establish a national policy on housing for disabled people (nor has HUD ever developed one), it does not affirm for disabled people a right to housing, and it contains no provisions for meeting the special needs of different disability groups.

Transportation

The Urban Mass Transportation Act of 1964, as amended, requires "special efforts" in planning and designing mass transportation facilities and services so they will be accessible to disabled people and states that it shall be a national policy for mass transportation to be available to all Americans. But "special efforts" is not defined, no enforcement is provided for, and no requirement for development of a national policy appears. DOT regulations specify that "special efforts" means "genuine, good-faith progress," without explaining what that means or requiring specific steps for accessibility. Rather than define, the regulations provide examples, which are helpful in offering direction but useless as enforcement tools. Large loopholes permit extensive renovations to be made in facilities and services without accessibility being mandated.

The National Mass Transportation Assistance Act (P. L. 93–503) provides for half-fare rates during non-peak hours for disabled and elderly passengers in all mass transportation projects receiving federal funds. While helpful, this provision is limited in its effectiveness because most mass transit remains largely inaccessible to many disabled individuals and because it is of little help in overcoming barriers to employment for disabled people.

The Amtrak Improvement Act of 1973 (P. L. 93–140) authorizes, but does not require, provisions for accessibility in intercity rail passenger service. The authorization specifically excludes commuter and other short-haul service, meaning that the law offers little help to disabled job seekers and workers. With the assistance of the Architectural and Transportation Barriers Compliance Board, Amtrak recently made its Amcafe cars accessible and is beginning renovations in several of its stations.

The Federal-Aid Highway Act of 1973 (P. L. 93–87), together with the 1974 amendments (P. L. 93–643), requires planning, design, construction, and operation under Highway Trust Fund moneys to include provisions for accessibility, including the requirement that all streets built with federal funds be equipped with curb-cuts or ramps at intersections.

Air travel remained free of any specific legislative requirements for accessibility until July, 1976, when the Airport and Airway Development Act Amendments (P. L. 94–352) mandated accessibility provisions in all new airport terminals and in all renovations. Individual pilots still have the authority to deny transportation at their discretion.

8

To Live a Life

The October, 1975, issue of *Developmental Medicine and Child Neurology,* a respected journal for physicians specializing in treatment of children who have mental and behavioral disorders, carried an editorial proposing greater selectivity by physicians in correcting "Nature's mistakes." Noting the limitations in financial and personnel resources available for diagnosis, treatment, education, rehabilitation, and life-long care for disabled individuals, the editorial argued that lavish care for one child means that other children may not receive assistance and that modern medicine's increasing sophistication in saving the lives of many infants who would have died in previous decades was compounding the problem daily. Recognizing that on this plan some nondisabled infants might be sacrificed needlessly, the author yearns for the day when political, moral, and religious prejudices will cease to shackle medical practice by requiring that all possible efforts be made to save a life.

Indeed, hospital care for a severely disabled child may cost in excess of $80,000 annually. Institutionalization costs are very high also. When lost taxes on wages never earned, lost economic stimulation on purchases never made, and lost productiveness in work and community participation never effected are included, the costs skyrocket. And the costs in human suffering, family disruption, and related intangibles are incalculable.

Do disabled people in fact have a right to live? If so, what is meant by the word "live"? Does it refer to mere survival or to a certain quality of life? And what does it mean to be alive in America today when medical care is exorbitantly expensive, when an adequate education is not available at any price, when housing cannot be located, when jobs are impossible to find, when isolation from normal human intercourse is imposed by communication and architectural barriers, when respect from others is rarely achieved and respect for one's self impossible to maintain, when self-determination and autonomy are as elusive and remote as are miraculous cures, when fraud and victimization are ever-present, and, yes, when media carry stories suggesting that you and the rest of America would be better off were you dead?

What does it do to people when they must struggle each and every day to overcome oppressive barriers? And what would it mean were these walls to come tumbling down? What is the answer and how do we find it? Is the issue one of money and priorities, ethics and charity, politics and power, attitudes and feelings, rights and wrongs, bricks and mortar, science and technology? Who will make the recommendations and who will decide?

Listen to a woman, 29 years old, living with her parents in rural Georgia:

I have always been an ambitious person—wanted to live alone, support myself. That dream has crumbled. I am not a viable person. I feel I am not useful. I am not satisfied. I feel I should be doing something but I don't know what.

And to an older man living with his sister-in-law:

I can't do anything for myself and I have no money. I need a new wheelchair; this one is falling apart. I wish they [VR] would help me get my mail. My family asked for help from the Post Office. I've sent letters all the way to Tennessee to the government. I can't get delivery because I'm off the road and the truck won't come in. It's not but a couple hundred feet but my sister is too old to walk up the road and I can't, so I have to wait for someone to bring it. In bad weather, I just wait and wait. I'd be so happy if the driver would pull in here.

A 52-year-old woman from New York:

Well, I can't go out for too long or go too far because if I have to go [to the toilet] I don't want to be embarrassed. So I just sit here in the wheelchair looking almost like a human being.

A younger woman from Maryland:

I hope I don't live too long. My son [16 years old] has his life to live and I don't want to be a burden on him. If I could win the lottery I would like to buy a nice little house somewhere and have someone cook and clean for me.

A man, in a wheelchair, from Ohio:

Why don't they have some way to cheaply answer the telephone without having to run for it?

A woman from Idaho:

I was born with C. P. [cerebral palsy] 49 years ago. I only went to the sixth grade in school. About five years ago, I found I could type on an electric typewriter. Well, I knew I couldn't afford to get one as I live off the state, so I asked a lot of clubs in my city if they would help me get one. They all turned me down flat. I got mad and had a nephew write a letter to the Governor of Idaho. I explained how things were and I told him I was tired of being put down by everyone just because I'm in a wheelchair. Most of my family just laughed and said he wouldn't even read my letter. Two weeks later I got a letter from the Governor saying I would have my typewriter within the next two weeks. Sure enough, two weeks later here the I.B.M. company came with a very good used I.B.M. electric typewriter that they had done over. No one will ever know how much I've enjoyed it. It seems so good to be able to write my own letters. I write poems and short stories. I have had two stories and also two poems published. I did some typing for Senator Frank Church of Idaho last fall. I know I make a few mistakes but I can only use my right hand as the other one is uncontrollable.

An Indiana woman:

Has anyone figured out how to take down and put up curtains and drapes from a wheelchair?

A man from California:

It makes my blood boil to see these no-good deaf-and-dumb beggars selling those alphabet cards. I bet half of 'em aren't even deaf either. I raised three kids, worked two jobs, repaired my own car and my own house, and I hear nothing at all. My friends have cards that mock those alphabet cards. They say: "I'm hearing. Please give what you can." On the other side is the phonetic alphabet. But that's not the answer either. Sometimes I wonder if the biggest problem deaf people have is hearing people or if it's other deaf people.

A man from Washington, D.C.:

The only problem blind people have is sighted people. We can do anything they can. But they won't let us.

A woman from Tennessee:

I was asked to give a talk before the Nurses' Association on "How I Have Lived with Multiple Sclerosis." Although it was not intentional on my part, a lesson was brought home to the nurses in that the seminar was held in an upstairs room, no elevators, and I was not able to climb the stairs and give my talk.

A man from Nevada:

People are always asking me how I live. And I know the real question is why.

Beginning

The barriers confronting disabled people are immense and inextricably intertwined. But one central problem seems to underlie most of these obstacles and that is the problem of right. For the fact is that disabled people most desire, I believe, only what is available to Americans who are not disabled. The requests—they are becoming demands now, after two hundred years of patience—are for the simple right to live, to learn, to work, to determine their own goals and life-styles, to earn the respect of others and their own self-respect, to obtain housing, to secure transportation, to receive needed treatment, to enjoy cultural and entertainment offerings. In the words of the Supreme Court in its *Papachriston* v. *City of Jacksonville* decision: "Independence and self-confidence, the feeling of creativity . . . , lives of high spirits rather than hushed, suffocating silence."

Yet rights are intensely personal things. It is possible to legislate rights and this has been done. But while rights are proposed as absolutes, they become reality only after political struggles. And in this struggle people come to perceive their lives differently. They see what could not be seen before and then, only then, does their behavior begin to change. Much later, what was once hotly disputed becomes accepted as simply human. This will happen, I believe, with disabled people as they seek their right, not to be human, but to be treated that way.

It is beginning now. Disabled people are starting to advocate for the rights they know someday will be theirs. Taking their cue from a March 16, 1827, *Freedom's Journal* editorial, they are saying: "We wish to plead our own causes. Too long have others spoken for us." The tragedy is that for two hundred years disabled people have not been asked about their needs and desires. Buildings went up before their inaccessibility was "discovered"—and then it was too late. During America's periods of greatest growth, when subways were constructed, television and motion pictures produced, telephone lines laid, school programs designed, and jobs manufactured disabled people were hidden away in attics, "special" programs, and institutions, unseen and their voices unheard. Day by day, year by year, America became ever more oppressive to its hidden minority. Even now, in the last quarter of the twentieth century, most of America remains blissfully unaware of the colossal dimensions of Handicapping America. The consciousness that must precede action remains for the future.

I am convinced disabled people will succeed, as blacks and women have before them, in raising the consciousness of America to their needs, problems, concerns—and to their abilities. For ultimately, that is what will be needed. It is not charity or public assistance, it is not a welfare state, it is not perpetual childhood that disabled people seek but the opportunity to develop and apply their abilities to the furthest reaches of their potentials. This will happen when businessmen recognize the contributions disabled workers can make, contributions they cannot now see. It will happen when educators perceive instruction as much a matter of nurturing strengths as alleviating weaknesses. It will happen when legislators conceive laws not to pacify disabled activists with symbolic language but to solve problems with enforceable requirements. It will happen, in the end, when the average citizen looks at a woman in a wheelchair, a man with a hearing aid, a child with crutches, not as people who can't but as people who can, seeing not the chrome and wires and wood so much as the individual and unique qualities that make someone human. It will happen, in the words of Robert Kennedy, when people ask not "Why?" but "Why not?"

The questions they ask on their way to "Why not?" will be tough ones with few easy answers. For rehabilitating America today is not the relatively simple problem it could have been two hundred years ago. The changes that will be necessary are frighteningly enormous, almost too large to comprehend much less to implement. We are talking about retrofitting an entire society, renovating buildings and subways, altering entrenched bureaucracies, and, perhaps most difficult of all, changing people themselves. But it must be done.

The process will be a slow one. It has begun that way.

The first tentative steps toward equality for disabled people are being taken in education, rehabilitation, employment, housing, transportation, and civil rights. We are beginning to appreciate the fact that there exists in this country a vast resource of virtually untapped energy and creativity, vision and productivity, potential and power. We are beginning to see that it is within our capacity to use these resources, slowly, perhaps but surely and steadily. We are beginning to understand that America handicaps disabled people. And we are beginning to realize that by freeing abilities from the shackles of disabilities, we are rehabilitating not only disabled people but America itself.

Appendix A ORGANIZATIONS

OF AND FOR DISABLED PEOPLE*

American Coalition of Citizens with Disabilities, Inc.
1346 Connecticut Avenue, N.W., Suite 817
Washington, D.C. 20036

A nationwide umbrella association of 65 organizations of and for disabled individuals, the Coalition works for full realization of the human and civil rights of people who have physical, mental, and emotional disabilities.

American Council of the Blind
1211 Connecticut Avenue, N.W., Suite 506
Washington, D.C. 20036

Promotes legislative and governmental advances enhancing the lives of blind individuals.

American Foundation for the Blind
15 West 16th Street
New York, New York 10011

Promotes integration of blind persons into the social, cultural, and economic life of the community.

American Speech and Hearing Association
10801 Rockville Pike
Rockville, Maryland 20850

* Adapted from *Directory of Organizations Interested in the Handicapped*, People to People Program, Suite 610, LaSalle Building, Connecticut and L Streets, N.W., Washington, D.C. 20036. 1976 edition.

Encourages scientific study in speech pathology and audiology, facilitates communication between professionals in these fields, and fosters improvement of clinical techniques.

Blinded Veterans Association
1735 DeSales Street, N.W.
Washington, D.C. 20036

Assists blinded veterans overcome educational, employment, and daily living problems.

Council for Exceptional Children
1920 Association Drive
Reston, Virginia 22091

Conducts research and training on education of disabled children and youth, promotes communication between specialists serving these students, and works for improved education legislation and services.

Council of State Administrators of Vocational Rehabilitation
1522 K Street, N.W., Suite 610
Washington, D.C. 20005

Serves as a resource for communication and cooperation between specialists working in the area of vocational rehabilitation of disabled youth and adults.

Disabled American Veterans
National Headquarters
P.O. Box 14301
Cincinnati, Ohio 45214

Promotes the welfare of service-connected disabled veterans.

Disability Rights Center
1346 Connecticut Ave. N.W.
Washington, D.C. 20036

Advocates on behalf of disabled applicants and employees in an effort to secure full implementation of Section 501 of the Rehabilitation Act of 1973.

Epilepsy Foundation of America
1828 L Street, N.W.
Washington, D.C. 20036

Advocates for persons with epilepsy.

Goodwill Industries of America
9200 Wisconsin Avenue, N.W.
Washington, D.C. 20014
Offers training in sheltered workshop settings for severely disabled individuals.

Human Resources Center
Willets Road
Albertson, New York 11507
Conducts research and training in special education and rehabilitation of severely disabled persons.

Muscular Dystrophy Associations of America, Inc.
810 Seventh Avenue
New York, New York 10019
Fosters research into cures and treatment for muscular dystrophy and related neuromuscular diseases.

National Association for Retarded Citizens
2709 Avenue E East, POB 6109
Arlington, Texas 76011
Furthers research, training, clinical practice, and education for mentally retarded children and adults.

National Association of the Deaf
814 Thayer Avenue
Silver Spring, Maryland 20910
Serves as a clearinghouse and citizen advocate in matters relating to deafness and hearing impairment.

National Association of the Physically Handicapped
2810 Terrace Road, S.E.
Apartment A-465
Washington, D.C. 20020
Promotes the economic, physical, and social well-being of physically disabled persons.

National Congress of Organizations of the Physically Handicapped, Inc.
6106 North 30 Street
Arlington, Virginia 22207

> Works for employment, education, equal rights, and rehabilitation of physically disabled individuals.

National Easter Seal Society for Crippled Children and Adults
2023 West Ogden Avenue
Chicago, Illinois 60612

> A federation of local facilities serving disabled persons and their families.

National Foundation/March of Dimes
1275 Mamaroneck Avenue
White Plains, New York 10605

> Works for prevention of birth defects.

National Multiple Sclerosis Society
205 East 42nd Street
New York, New York 10010

> Supports research on the central nervous system, educates lay and professional persons about multiple sclerosis, and coordinates information dissemination about the disease.

National Paraplegia Foundation
333 North Michigan Avenue
Chicago, Illinois 60601

> Stimulates research, training, and treatment in the area of spinal cord injury.

National Rehabilitation Association
1522 K Street, N.W.
Washington, D.C. 20005

> Facilitates communication between professionals working with disabled youth and adults.

Paralyzed Veterans of America
7315 Wisconsin Avenue, N.W.
Washington, D.C. 20014

Focuses upon improving programs of medicine and rehabilitation for veteran and nonveteran adults with spinal cord injuries.

Teletypewriters for the Deaf, Inc.
POB 28332
Washington, D.C. 20005

Publishes a directory of TTY numbers to improve communication between deaf people via telephone.

United Cerebral Palsy Associations, Inc.
66 East 34th Street
New York, New York 10016

Seeks solutions to the multiple health, personal, social, and employment problems of persons who have cerebral palsy.

Appendix B GOVERNMENT

PROGRAMS FOR DISABLED PEOPLE

INFORMATION AND REFERRAL

Office of Handicapped Individuals
Office for Human Development
U.S. Department of Health, Education, and Welfare
200 Independence Avenue, S.W.
Washington, D.C. 20201

> A coordinating and advocacy unit which operates a general-purpose clearinghouse on disability program information. A good place to start.

"Closer Look"
The National Information Center for the Handicapped
1201 16th Street, N.W., Suite 607E
Washington, D.C. 20036

> Provides parents of disabled children and youth with information about special education through "Closer Look" advertisements and commercials and through several publications.

President's Committee on Employment of the Handicapped
1111 20th Street, N.W., Suite 636
Washington, D.C. 20036

> Offers information about vocational preparation and employment of disabled persons and publishes the periodical "Disabled USA."

President's Committee on Mental Retardation
7th and D Streets, S.W.
Washington, D.C. 20202

Coordinates government efforts on behalf of and offers information about retarded individuals.

EDUCATION AND REHABILITATION

Bureau of Education for the Handicapped
Office of Education
U.S. Department of Health, Education, and Welfare
Donohue Building
Washington, D.C. 20202

Sponsors special education programs on the preschool, elementary, secondary, and postsecondary levels. Trains teachers and support personnel and funds research on education for disabled persons.

Rehabilitation Services Administration
Office of Human Development
U.S. Department of Health, Education, and Welfare
330 C Street, S.W.
Washington, D.C. 20201

Sponsors vocational training programs and facilities, trains counselors and other rehabilitation personnel, and funds research.

Developmental Disabilities Office
Office of Human Development
U.S. Department of Health, Education, and Welfare
330 C Street, S.W.
Washington, D.C. 20201

Coordinates and advocates on behalf of persons with autism, cerebral palsy, epilepsy, and mental retardation.

Vocational Rehabilitation for Disabled Veterans
Veterans Administration
Washington, D.C. 20420

Trains disabled veterans for employment.

Home Economics Education for the Handicapped
Extension Service
U.S. Department of Agriculture
Washington, D.C. 20250

>   Administers state programs helping families adjust to disability

EMPLOYMENT AND CIVIL RIGHTS

Employment and Training Administration
U.S. Department of Labor
600 D Street, S.W.
Washington, D.C. 20201

>   Sponsors state employment services, sheltered workshops, and public service employment programs for disabled persons.

Office of Federal Contracts Compliance Programs
Employment Standards Administration
U.S. Department of Labor
600 D Street, S.W.
Washington, D.C. 20201

>   Administers Section 503 of the Rehabilitation Act of 1973.

Office of the Secretariat
Interagency Committee on Handicapped Employees
Civil Service Commission
1900 E Street, N.W.
Washington, D.C. 20415

>   Administers Section 501 of the Rehabilitation Act of 1973, which affects federal employment of disabled persons.

Office for Civil Rights
Office of the Secretary
U.S. Department of Health, Education, and Welfare
330 Independence Avenue, S.W.
Washington, D.C. 20201

>   Administers Section 504 of the Rehabilitation Act for HEW and coordinates the federal effort pursuant to Section 504.

TRANSPORTATION

Urban Mass Transportation Administration
U.S. Department of Transportation
400 7th Street, S.W.
Washington, D.C. 20590

Regulates mass transit (bus, subway) programs.

Federal Aviation Administration
U.S. Department of Transportation
400 7th Street, S.W.
Washington, D.C. 20590

Regulates air travel by disabled persons.

Architectural and Transportation Barriers Compliance Board
Office of Human Development
U.S. Department of Health, Education, and Welfare
330 C Street, S.W.
Washington, D.C. 20201

Administers Section 502 of the Rehabilitation Act of 1973.

Veterans Administration
Washington, D.C. 20420

Provides direct payments for purchase and/or alteration of automobiles and other conveyance for disabled veterans.

HOUSING

Office of the Secretary
U.S. Department of Housing and Urban Development
451 7th Street, S.W.
Washington, D.C. 20410

Administers Section 8 and Section 202 programs for housing disabled persons, offers loans for construction and renovation, and regulates public and private housing programs serving disabled people.

Veterans Administration
Washington, D.C. 20420

Provides direct payments for housing for disabled veterans, particularly those with paraplegia.

HEALTH AND SOCIAL SERVICES

Bureau of Disability Insurance
Social Security Administration
U.S. Department of Health, Education, and Welfare
6401 Security Boulevard
Baltimore, Maryland 21235

> Administers cash payment programs for disabled individuals and their dependents.

Bureau of Supplementary Security Income
Social Security Administration
U.S. Department of Health, Education, and Welfare
108 West High Drive
Baltimore, Maryland 21235

> Administers the SSI program.

Bureau of Health Insurance
Room 700, East Highrise
Social Security Administration
U.S. Department of Health, Education, and Welfare
Baltimore, Maryland 21235

> Administers the Medicare program.

Division of Mental Health Service Programs
National Institute of Mental Health
U.S. Department of Health, Education, and Welfare
5600 Fishers Lane
Rockville, Maryland 20852

> Supports mental health facilities.

Crippled Children's Services
Bureau of Community Health Services
Public Health Service
U.S. Department of Health, Education, and Welfare
5600 Fishers Lane
Rockville, Maryland 20852

> Administers state programs serving mobility-limited children and youth.

Veterans Administration
Washington, D.C. 20420

Provides nursing home, domiciliary, outpatient, hospitalization, prosthetics, state hospital, and hospital-based home care for disabled veterans.

SPECIAL PROGRAMS

American Printing House for the Blind
1839 Frankfort Avenue
Louisville, Kentucky 40206

Publishes and distributes "talking books," brailled texts, embossed books, and large-type texts.

Gallaudet College
7th Street and Florida Avenue, N.E.
Washington, D.C. 20002

Provides higher education for deaf persons. Also features model preschool, elementary, secondary, and continuing education programs, and trains workers with deaf persons.

Division for the Blind and Physically Handicapped
Library of Congress
Washington, D.C. 20542

Provides free library services through 140 cooperating libraries for blind and physically disabled persons who cannot benefit from regular type.

Notes

Rather than burden the reader with numerous reference citations and irksome interruptions of the narrative, I have chosen to document most sources in the text itself when readability would not be impaired. Because this is a book written for general as well as specialized audiences, secondary rather than primary sources are stressed here and in the References. In the Notes that follow, the numerals to the left of each entry are page numbers.

Chapter 1. First Thoughts

2 - 16. On historical antecedents, see Bronowski (1973), Hawkes and Woolley (1963), and Telford and Sawrey (1972).

17. The Social Security Administration Survey of Disabled Adults was reported in a series of monographs available from SSA's Baltimore headquarters. See, especially, Allan and Cinsky (1972).

18. During 1974 and 1975 the Urban Institute (2100 M Street, N.W., Washington, D.C. 20037) conducted a "Comprehensive Service Needs Study" of individuals who were severely disabled. The 854-page final report of this RSA-funded study is a major source of information on independent living rehabilitation. The project was directed by Jerry Turem.

22 - 23. For brief and readable summaries of some of Kleck's and Tringo's work, see *Psychology Today*, November 1975, 122, 124.

27. The Travis quote is from Alexander (1974), 77.

28. See Turem (1975) on "confusion of priorities."

30. Laski (1976), 12.

35 - 36. The examples of independent living problems are adapted from

items appearing in *Accent on Living* (1974–1976 volumes) as letters to the editor and news briefs, and from personal communications to the author. *Accent on Living*, which is edited by Raymond Cheever, is available at POB 700, Gillum Road and High Drive, Bloomington, Illinois 61701.
37. The New York *Post*, July 13, 1976, 2.

Chapter 2. Ability and Disability

41 - 42. On susceptibility, see Rabkin and Streuning (1976).
43 - 44, 48 - 49, 53 - 54, 58 - 59, 63 - 64, 66. On the neurology and physiology of disability, see in particular Young (1971). *Psychology Today: An Introduction* (CRM Books, 1970) contains good basic descriptions.

Chapter 3. You Can't Get There from Here

76. On the design of buildings, see Heyer (1966).
77. The NCAB study is summarized in Nugent (1977).
82. On General Motors and TRANSBUS, see "GM Puts Brakes on 'Bus of the Future' " in *Environmental Action*, August 28, 1976, 9–11. The Shapiro quote is from *Accent on Living*, Fall 1976, 21.
83. The Stanford study is discussed in the *Environmental Action* story just cited.
87. Accessibility features of airports are listed in *Access Travel* (1976), a publication of the Architectural and Transportation Barriers Compliance Board, Washington, D.C. 20201.
91. Allison's testimony appears in *Freedom of Choice* (1975), also published by the ATBCB.
92. Pickett's efforts are described in Newhouse (1977).

Chapter 4. Us and Them

112 - 118. Roger Brown's *Social Psychology* (1965) is an excellent source on attitudes.
123 - 124. On "inferior" status, see Yuker (1977).

Chapter 5. No Right to Learn

134 - 135. Katherine Jamieson's story is adapted from a short article by de Boor (1975).
139 - 140. The learning disability film study was done by Foster, et al. (1976).
140. The Hobbs (1975) quote is from page 15.
146 - 147. Phyllis Bowe, personal communication, March 16, 1975.

149. On placement, see Telford and Sawrey (1972).
153 - 154. The CEC definition appears on page 255 of Council for Exceptional Children (1977).

Chapter 7. To Right the Wrongs

185 - 188. The examples are adapted from items appearing in *Accent on Living* (1974–1976) as letters to the editor and news briefs and from personal communications.
203 - 204. DOL, personal communication, March 14, 1977, Conference sponsored by President's Committee on Employment of the Handicapped, and Eunice Fiorito, personal communication, August 15, 1976.
208. From "Jimmy Carter on Americans with Disabilities," press release of September 22, 1976.

Chapter 8. To Live a Life

220 - 223. Examples are taken from Turem (1975) and from pieces of personal communication (undated) from the persons whose comments are cited.
223. Supreme Court, 405 U.S. 156,164 (1972).

References

Access Travel. Washington, D.C.: Architectural and Transportation Barriers Compliance Board, 1976.

Achtenberg, J. " 'Crips' Unite to Enforce Symbolic Laws." *University of San Fernando Valley Law Review,* Fall 1975.

Adorno, T., Frenkel-Brunswick, E., Levinson, D., and Sanford, R. *The Authoritarian Personality.* New York: Harper, 1950.

Alexander, B. "Disabled Barred from College?" *Accent on Living,* Spring 1974.

Allan, K., and Cinsky, M. *General Characteristics of the Disabled Population.* Report Number 19, Social Security Survey of the Disabled: 1966. Washington, D.C.: U.S. Department of Health, Education, and Welfare, 1972.

Allison, L. Written testimony. *Freedom of Choice.* Washington, D.C.: Architectural and Transportation Barriers Compliance Board, 1975, 74–76.

American National Standards Institute. *American National Standard Specifications to Make Buildings and Facilities Accessible to and Usable by the Physically Handicapped.* New York: The Institute, 1961.

Anderson, J., and Whitten, L. "Handicapped Plan 10-City Sit-in." Washington *Post,* March 26, 1977, E 37.

Berkowitz, M. *Cost Burden of Disabilities and Effects of Federal Program Expenditures.* Final report. New Brunswick, N.J.: Disability and Health Economics Research, Bureau of Economic Research, Rutgers University, 1974.

Bowe, F. "Looking Beyond the Disabilities." *Worklife,* May 1977, 13–15.

Bronowski, J. *The Ascent of Man.* Boston: Little, Brown, 1973.

Brown, R. *Social Psychology.* New York: Free Press, 1965.

Butler, R. *Why Survive? Old Age in America.* New York: Harper & Row, 1975.

Carter, J. *Jimmy Carter on Americans with Disabilities.* Atlanta: Democratic Presidential Campaign Committee, 1976.

Colbert, J., Kalisk, R., and Chang, P. "Two Psychological Portals of Entry for Disadvantaged Groups." *Rehabilitation Literature,* July 1973, 194–202.

Conley, R. W. *The Economics of Mental Retardation.* Baltimore: Johns Hopkins University Press, 1974.

Council for Exceptional Children. "Full Educational Opportunities for Handicapped Individuals." *Awareness Papers.* Washington, D.C.: White House Conference on Handicapped Individuals, 1977.

de Boor, M. "What Is to Become of Katherine?" *Exceptional Children,* May 1975, 517–518.

Ellison, R. *Invisible Man.* New York: Random House, 1952.

Foster, G. F., Schmidt, C. R. and Sabatino, D. Teacher Expectations and the Label Learning Disabilities, *Journal of Learning Disabilities,* Volume 9, 111–114, (1976).

Fried, J. "Neurotransmitters—Messengers of the Brain." *Reader's Digest,* December 1976.

Frolich, P. "Income of the Newly Disabled." *Social Security Bulletin,* September 1975.

Gailis, A., and Susman, K. "Abroad in the Land: Legal Strategies to Effectuate the Rights of the Physically Disabled." *Georgetown Law Review,* July 1973.

General Accounting Office. *Training Educators for the Handicapped: A Need to Redirect Federal Programs.* Washington, D.C.: Author, 1976.

Gilhool, T. "The Uses of the Courts and of Lawyers: Towards Realizing the Rights of Citizens Who Are Different." In Kugel, R., and Shearer, A., eds. *Changing Patterns in Residential Services for the Mentally Retarded.* Washington, D.C.: President's Committee on Mental Retardation, 1976.

"GM Puts Brakes on 'Bus of the Future.'" *Environmental Action,* August 28, 1976.

Goldenson, R., ed. *The Disability Handbook.* New York: McGraw-Hill, 1977.

Gollay, E., and Bennett, A. *The College Guide for Students with Disabilities.* Cambridge, Mass.: Abt Associates, 1976.

Harrington, M. *The Other America.* New York: Macmillan, 1962.

Hawkes, J., and Woolley, C. *History of Mankind: Prehistory and the Beginnings of Civilization.* New York: Harper & Row, 1963.

Heddinger, R. "The Twelve Year Battle for a Barrier Free METRO." *American Rehabilitation,* May–June 1976.

Heyer, P. *Architects on Architecture.* New York: Walker and Company, 1966.

Hobbs, N. *The Futures of Children: Categories, Labels, and Their Consequences.* Report of the Project on Classification of Exceptional Children. San Francisco: Jossey-Bass, 1975.

Laski, F. "Legal Advocacy, Positive Factor in Rights for Disabled People." *American Rehabilitation,* May–June 1976.

Laurie, G. *Housing and Home Services for the Disabled.* Hagerstown, Md.: Harper & Row, 1977.

Lenihan, J. "Disabled Americans: A History." *Performance,* November–December 1976–January 1977, whole.

Liebergott, H. "Reason the Need: Some Thoughts on the Necessity for Changing Attitudes toward Handicapped People." Mimeo, 1976. Available from author, Bureau of Education for the Handicapped.

Millstead, T. "The Right to Work." *Accent on Living,* Winter 1974/75, 51–54.

Nagy, K. "Special Human Services Are Part of Our Human Concept." *Rehabilitation Literature,* June 1975.

Newhouse, E. "Paralyzed Woodworker Builds His Own House." *Washington Star,* January 7, 1977, F-7.

Nugent, T. "Architectural Accessibility." *Awareness Papers.* Washington, D.C.: White House Conference on Handicapped Individuals, 1977.

Olympus Research Corporation. *Assessment of Vocational Education Programs for the Handicapped Under Part B of the 1968 Amendments to the Vocational Education Act.* Salt Lake City: Author, 1975.

Ozer, M. "Screening, Diagnosis, and Early Intervention." Paper prepared for White House Conference on Handicapped Individuals. Mimeo, 1977.

Performance of Physically Impaired Workers in Manufacturing Industries. Labor Statistics Bulletin Number 923. Washington, D.C.: Department of Labor, 1948.

Porter, S. "Economics of Rehabilitation." Jackson *Daily News,* October 18, 1976, 18A.

Psychology Today: An Introduction. Del Mar, Calif.: Communications, Research, Machines, 1970.

Rabkin, J., and Streuning, E. "Life Events, Stress, and Illness." *Science,* December 3, 1976.

Sands, H., and Zalkind, S. "Effects of an Educational Campaign to Change Employer Attitudes Toward Epileptics. *Epilepsia,* January 1972.

Scheingold, S. *The Politics of Right.* New Haven: Yale University Press, 1974.

Stanford Research Institute, *TRANSBUS Report.* Washington, D.C.: Department of Commerce, 1976.

Telford, C., and Sawrey, J. *The Exceptional Individual.* Englewood Cliffs, N.J.: Prentice-Hall, 1972.

Ten Broek, J. "The Right to Live in the World: The Disabled in the Law of Torts." *California Law Review,* 1966, 841.

Turem, J., ed. *Report of the Comprehensive Service Needs Study.* Washington, D.C.: The Urban Institute, 1975.

Vietorisz, T., Mier, R., and Harrison, B. "Full Employment at Living Wages." *Annals of the American Academy of Political and Social Science,* 1975.

Williams, A. "Is Hiring the Handicapped Good Business?" *Journal of Rehabilitation,* March–April 1972.

Young, J. *An Introduction to the Study of Man.* London: Oxford University Press, 1971.

Yuker, H. E. "Attitudes of the General Public Toward Handicapped Individuals." *Awareness Papers.* Washington, D.C.: White House Conference on Handicapped Individuals, 1977.

Zellweger, H. "Modern Medical Problems." *Developmental Medicine and Child Neurology,* October 1975, 561–562.

Index